BMW

RACING MOTORCYCLES

THE MASTERY OF SPEED

BMW

RACING MOTORCYCLES

THE MASTERY OF SPEED

LAUREL C. ALLEN AND MARK GARDINER

Whitehorse Press
Center Conway, New Hampshire

We recognize that some words, model names and designations mentioned herein are the property of the trademark holder. We use them for identification purposes only.

Whitehorse Press books are also available at discounts in bulk quantity for sales and promotional use. For details about special sales or for a catalog of motorcycling books, videos, and gear write to the publisher:

Whitehorse Press
107 East Conway Road
Center Conway, New Hampshire 03813
Phone: 603-356-6556 or 800-531-1133
E-mail: CustomerService@WhitehorsePress.com
Internet: www.WhitehorsePress.com

ISBN: 978-1-884313-65-3

5 4 3 2 1

Printed in China

ACKNOWLEDGEMENTS

The authors gratefully acknowledge the permission granted by BMW Group and BMW Mobile Tradition for use of images from their company archives. Those organizations supplied all images used in this book, except for the following:

Artemis Images, www.artemisimages.com, page 154
Ian Falloon, page 107
Mark Gardiner, page 175
Mick Woollett, page 114
Neale Bayly, page 174
Rob O'Brien, pages 162, 165
Speedbrain, page 159
Tom Riles, pages 115, 116, 118, 119, 121, 122, 123, 147, 149, 151
Udo Gietl, pages 108, 109, 111, 120

The authors would also like to acknowledge the role of Fred Jakobs, historian and archivist for BMW Mobile Tradition in Munich, who read through the text and applied his encyclopedic knowledge in making some welcomed corrections and suggestions.

Finally, special thanks go to Laurence Kuykendall at BMW North America, whose vision to share the remarkable story of his dynamic company and its superlative motorcycles made this book possible.

Table of Contents

Introduction

There it sits, on the floor of the annual Berlin car show: a gleaming motorcycle whose every detail testifies to a history of unparalleled innovation. The presence of a transversely mounted boxer-twin engine marks the machine as a BMW, and from the elegance of its shaft-driven design to the solidity of its twin-triangle frame, it's built to make history.

In fact, those with a poetic nature could fairly label this motorcycle "heaven-sent," as several of the minds involved in its creation and manufacture were the same ones responsible for powering airplanes to world-record-setting altitudes just a few years before. Given a few seasons, however, this newest creation will eclipse them all, evolving into a line of motorcycles that will collect, in just over the next decade, 76 world records and too many trophies to count.

The machine is an R 32. The year is 1923. BMW's racing legacy—which will define the company's reputation as a premier marque while fueling astounding, brand-sustaining technological advances—is about to begin.

Dreams of flight crash to the ground

Though it says something remarkable when a company has existed long enough to be shaped by two World Wars, it probably didn't strike BMW Managing Director Franz Josef Popp as particularly glorious when the historic 1919 signing of the Treaty of Versailles made airplane manufacturing forbidden in Germany, then a defeated power. BMW didn't just make airplane engines at the time; they were wholly devoted to making the best. The German military had ordered 2,000 BMW IIIa engines a year earlier, and the further-developed IV engine, in an aircraft piloted by Franz Zeno Diemer, set a 32,023-foot world record for altitude just three weeks before the Versailles treaty was ratified.

It was that record, however—the very one that Popp hoped would bring even greater success and

security to the company—that attracted the attention of the Allied Control Commission. The Allies promptly confiscated assets related to BMW's aero engine development, and it wasn't long before the once-proud Bavarian Motor Works was reduced to making everything from toolboxes to office equipment.

It couldn't have been an easy adjustment for any of the BMW staff; from the engineers to the men who did assembly work, all were accustomed to the exacting standards of the aero industry and literally did not know how to make a mediocre product. One can imagine, though, that the development hit prominent BMW designer Max Friz especially hard…. The man who was responsible for the cloud-piercing, record-breaking IV was now reduced to creating truck and boat engines from scrap.

But Friz, like BMW itself, would rise again; he'd returned to designing aircraft engines by 1924 and eventually became a director of BMW AG as well as the company's first chief designer. Along the way, however, Friz—whose passion was always for aircraft—was issued a more terrestrial

Max Friz' first love may have been airplane engines, but it was his engine work for BMW's first motorcycle—the R 32—that would change the company's future forever. In this 1918 photograph, Friz (at right) poses with Zeno Diemer (center), who's just completed his second successful flight in the BMW IIIa-powered plane.

< Franz Josef Popp had the talent and foresight to keep BMW adaptable throughout its early years. It was a characteristic that allowed the company to survive two World Wars.

The first advertisement for the R 32 appeared in the September 30, 1923 edition of Automobilwelt-Flugwelt. *The R 32 itself went slightly more cosmopolitan, making its debut at the 1923 Paris Salon.*

challenge: to build an entirely new motorcycle. His answer to that challenge changed BMW forever.

Friz converted the guest room of his house into a workshop and emerged four months later with the plans for the R 32, the first motorcycle ever to be labeled a BMW. Its engine was based on the M 2 B 15, a 500cc horizontally opposed twin-cylinder unit that BMW had manufactured for several years prior, but from there, Friz—always an innovator—had left the past behind.

Those who attended the 1923 Berlin Salon saw a side-valve, fully encased boxer-twin engine mounted across a steel-tube frame, fuel tank tucked underneath the top tubes, a front fork sprung by a quarter-elliptic leaf spring, and the long handle of a three-speed gearbox arcing toward a rider's right hand. Even those who were oblivious to the revolutionary absence of the traditional chain and sprocket drive could appreciate the solidity and aesthetics of the angular, black machine with flash white pin striping, and 1,500 customers lightened their wallets to own one before the end of the year. The R 32 was the star of the show and much talked about in the press the next day, but—although it was truly a BMW, from

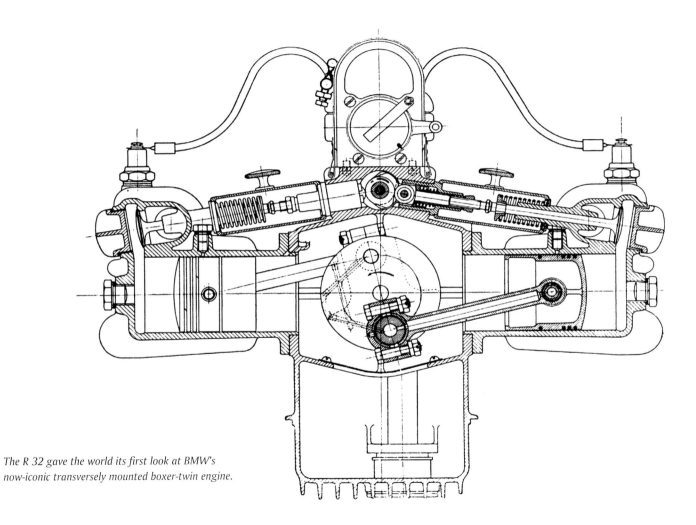

*The R 32 gave the world its first look at BMW's
now-iconic transversely mounted boxer-twin engine.*

Friz took his work seriously, doing much of the testing himself. Here he puts a racing version of the R 32—featuring steel cylinders and overhead-valve cylinder heads—through its paces in 1924.

>This restored R 32 is fitted with the standard side-valve heads, as evidenced by the position of the exhaust port, noticeably higher than the axis of the cylinder.

its engine to its price tag—it served, in the end, mostly as a harbinger of things to come.

War-torn Germany didn't experience the same sort of carefree "Golden Twenties" that the relatively untouched United States did, but it was still a time of rapid invention and technological progress, and the average city-dweller's life was changing quickly as advances in radio, transportation, film, and electricity brought more and more gadgets into their lives. Reliability—conspicuously absent from many of these inventions, particularly in modern forms of transportation—was highly valued, and the R 32 had it in spades. Though its top speed of more than 60 mph was merely respectable, the high quality of its construction put it in a different class altogether from most other motorcycles on the market. So how best to prove those qualities to the average consumer? If you were a manufacturer in the 1920s and '30s, there was only one answer: go racing.

Plenty of today's OEMs field race teams as part of their advertising strategy, but the power that race results have to sell motorcycles was perhaps never greater than it was then. While modern consumers often prove more influenced by sleek ad

campaigns than finishing-order, pre-WWII consumers traded news of race victories and race heroes with a fervor that could make or break a brand's reputation. It didn't matter that most of BMW's models were meant for touring, not racing; nothing proved brand superiority (and earned consumers' loyalty) better than a long line of trophies.

In Germany, as in other European nations at the time, competition was also actively encouraged by the ruling political party as a way to boost national pride. Add all that up and it was only natural that BMW would soon test its mettle against other manufacturers on the race circuit, and the highest prize of all—to those involved in politics, true, but especially to those who'd poured their lives into the BMW brand—was to beat foreign manufacturers on foreign soil, thus gaining entry to and prestige within international markets.

The R 32 had its supporters—*Der Motorwagen* magazine noted, "Despite its youth, it is a remarkably fast and successful motorcycle"—but those today who remember seeing their first BMW in a race paddock won't be surprised to hear that plenty of people were initially skeptical about the

R 32's chances of success, and further, that the doubters generally focused on exactly the same characteristic that can give some pause even now: the transversely mounted boxer-twin engine. It wasn't the function of the engine that was in question but rather how its protruding cylinders could possibly be practical for a race application. In 1923, skeptics predicted the engine would be easily damaged by even a minor tip-over; instead, BMW motorcycles turned out to be perhaps the most durable and dependable known to man.

In the model's first competitive outing at Solitude (a racing venue near Stuttgart), however, none of the three R 32s that started the race made it to the finish. What's worse, they were handily trumped by the creation of former BMW employee Martin Stolle, who—after leaving BMW the year before—had gone on to design an engine for the Victoria KR2, then the most successful German motorcycle in its class. With so much at stake, there was nothing for BMW to do but devote itself to a quick and triumphant return.

Serial production of the R 32 began in 1924, at BMW's Munich factory. Since most BMW employees had previously worked with airplane engines, exacting standards were par for the course.

Off to the great road races of Europe, and to Europe's great off-road races

When he crossed the BMW doorstep in 1922, 25-year-old Rudolf Schleicher was a graduate of the Munich College of Advanced Technology, an avid motorcyclist, and bright enough to be immediately put to work for Friz. When he retired from the company 38 years later, he was a legend.

Friz had tested the original R 32 by contending a sort of club race, but Schleicher was essentially the first in a long line of truly multi-talented BMW employees whose development work took place both in and outside the workshop. Engine designers, store owners, and retail salesmen all notched trophies for the brand as racers, and those who were hired to race professionally jumped from race tracks and road courses to off-road events and even hillclimbs with apparent ease. It was Schleicher, though, who brought home BMW's

>*The Rudolf Schleicher-designed R 37 was BMW's first entry into the sporting class. Although only 152 were built, they established BMW as a racing marque.*

The R 37 came about when Schleicher fitted aluminum heads with overhead valves to the proven R 32 design. It produced about 16 hp at 4,000 rpm, which was impressive in 1925. Complexity and high production cost made it a specialty item, but it served as proof-of-concept for many subsequent ohv designs.

>Rudi Reich—shown here at Solitude in 1924— went on to win the 500cc German National Championship that year.

21

first gold medal, aboard a revised R 32 powered by his M 2 B 35 engine.

Although a gold medal was significantly better than a triple DNF, it soon became clear that the M 2 B 35 wasn't destined to take over the world. Its fatal flaw was the tendency of its steel cylinder and monoblock head to overheat, making it no surprise that its victory came in the 1924 ADAC Winter Rally. But Schleicher had an ace in his pocket: two years earlier, he'd begun design of a light alloy cylinder head and an enclosed, lubricated, 90-degree overhead-valve system surrounded by circumferential cooling fins with passages. It was a revolutionary design (Schleicher quickly patented the fins), and by the time the R 37 went into limited production in 1925, the resulting 494cc M 2 B 36 engine put out 16 bhp—nearly twice that of the R 32—and benefited from BMW's new three-slide, 26mm carburetor.

The R 37's chassis was similar to the R 32's, though it now featured trailing link front suspension and an expanding shoe front brake. More importantly, its cylinders were turned from steel billet (and featured removable aluminum heads), and the overhead-valve design of the R 32 had been abandoned in favor of side valves. The R 37 was a surprisingly light 296 lbs considering its brazed steel frame, and it rolled along on 26-inch tires (2.5-inches wide in the front; 3 in the back). With a top speed of 71 mph, it was

>While the '23 Solitude event couldn't have been worse for BMW, the '24 event could not have been better. The R 37-mounted Franz Bieber, Rudi Reich, and Rudolf Schleicher (from left, with Schleicher off-camera) took victories in three classes.

BMW's first entry into the sporting class, and it was extremely expensive. Intended mainly for competitive use, only 152 R 37s were built during the model's limited-production run (which began in 1925), but by the time the R 37 was available for purchase, it had a pedigree that justified its price.

Following his 1924 ADAC outing, Schleicher had headed back to Solitude, the site of BMW's '23 debacle, with Rudi Reich and Franz Bieber. In stark contrast to the dismal results of the previous year, the trio took victory in three categories and Reich served notice of BMW's newfound competitiveness by notching the fastest time of the event. Their machines—which produced a claimed bhp of 22—also signaled the start of BMW's purpose-built race prototype program, which expanded to include ten very special R 37s that were used to test new engine and chassis designs even as they continued to amass victories.

On one such Schleicher-tuned prototype, Bieber underlined the brand's arrival on the racing scene by winning the 1924 500cc German National Championship for road racing. BMWs continued to score regular victories in various other German events throughout that year and the next—Josef Stelzer won the 1925 250cc national title while Reich found victory in the 500cc class, and BMWs won more than 100 national races in 1925 alone—but it was 1926 that made the rest of the racing world finally sit up and take notice. As a privateer entry with one friend and, unknowingly, the wrong rubber (in his book *The BMW Story*, Ian Falloon notes that the duo was "[a]lmost laughed out of the race" for contending the event on street tires), Schleicher earned a gold medal at the prestigious '26 International Six Days Trial in Great Britain. His friend, Friz Roth, won a silver.

Since the ISDT was widely held to be the most arduous event in the world of competitive motorcycle racing, Schleicher's stylish finish—*The Motorcycle* magazine observed that they couldn't find a single leak on the "beautifully quiet" machine—earned some highly valuable ink in foreign publications. But when the Grand Prix road racing series rolled into Germany that year, BMW's reputation as a maker of high-performance motorcycles was truly launched in international circles, as rider Paul Koppen laid down the fastest lap of the race on his way to overall victory. Rarely, if ever, had a marque accomplished so much in three short years.

By 1925—in only their second year of motorcycle production—BMW was logging wins in virtually every genre and class of racing available. Shown here is Josef Stelzer, winner of the '25 250cc national title, sitting on a 500cc R 37.

The rise of the Kompressor, the fall of records

While motorcycle racers' level of bravery will never be assessed at anything below "super-human," the men who lined up for races in the days before 1.5mm leather suits with internal armor, helmets with crumple-zone technology, and circuits lined with Airfence did so with the kind of courage that often strikes other people as madness. Some wore thin leather jackets belted at the waist (while others donned jerseys or sweaters), and head protection generally amounted to leather, beanie-sized helmets with a pair of goggles. Even a slow-speed crash could have dire consequences: broken bones, skull fractures, and death were all-too-common on the racing circuit. Still, there never was—and likely never will be—a shortage of souls who found life itself curled up inside high speeds, big risks, and the thrill of victory. Perhaps chief among

these in BMW history was Ernst Henne, who, at the age of 22, was signed in 1926 as one of BMW's first true factory riders.

An apprentice motor mechanic by age 14, Henne had a natural love of machines that led him to try his first race in 1923. Only three years later, he took sixth at the Monza European Grand Prix, catching the attention of BMW personnel. Henne accepted BMW's offer and lost little time in proving himself an excellent investment. Despite a practice crash that left him unconscious for nine days, Henne returned to competition in time to take the '26 500cc German national title—providing BMW its third consecutive win in the class—and became the 750cc German National Champion the year after. It's remarkable to realize that when seen in the context of Henne's overall legacy, those wins were little more than an auspicious beginning.

For motorsports enthusiasts in the 1920s, one of the most important races in Europe—some would argue *the* most important race in Europe—was the Targa Florio, held near Palermo in the Italian region of Sicily. It was also one of the most difficult events a motorcyclist could run: a 67-mile

< Record-breaking was an excellent way to gain publicity and unload motorcycles, and BMW's man for the job was Ernst Henne (at right). With 76 speed records to his name by the time he was done, it's likely Henne and Schleicher exchanged more than one congratulatory handshake.

Henne lines up on a #93 500cc machine (second row, left) in 1926.

>The Targa Floria was one of the most grueling and treacherous road races in the world. These two BMW R 57/63s—numbers 2 (Henne) and 5 (Köppen)— have three long 67-mile laps ahead of them.

course that included well over a thousand corners (many of them treacherous hairpins) and severe changes in altitude and climate. BMW historian Fred Jakobs reports that a single lap of the Targa Florio circuit—which was deemed too dangerous for any kind of competition by the international racing community in 1973—would have involved 2,000 hand-changes of the gearbox, at minimum.

BMW's first entry into the Targa Florio came in 1927, with German Grand Prix-winner Koppen as pilot. His surprise win was backed by Henne's '28 Targa Florio victory (this despite a punctured tube, which Henne calmly stopped to change), and Koppen retained Florio honors for BMW in 1929 by winning the race a second time, giving the brand three consecutive victories. The Targa Florio wins, however, meant more to BMW than just additional recognition on the world stage. In 1927, Schleicher had begun experimenting with and refining a technology that would usher in the company's most successful period to date, and the Targia Florio bikes represented BMW's first advances in supercharging.

After Schleicher left BMW in April of '27 (reportedly following an argument with Friz about

29

supercharging), it was left to Friz to carry out the development of the company's supercharging technology, but it is Henne who is perhaps most closely associated with supercharging since its emergence overlapped with Henne's own emerging passion for record-setting.

It was a passion that often looked like compulsion; it seemed Henne would go anywhere, as many times as necessary, to ride a two- or four-wheeled vehicle in any conditions and on any surface (ice included) if there was a record waiting for him at the end of the mile. Though his string of accomplishments is nearly as exhausting as it is inspiring to read about, Henne's unrelenting quest for records and intense overall drive correlated well with BMW's now-rampant development, which was fueled in large part by the dedication of Franz Josef Popp.

By this time, the R 37—BMW's first real race machine—had been replaced by the R 47. That was not a race-specific model, though a Werks-Rennmaschine ("Works Racer") version was produced. Its cases were stamped simply "WR 500" and it initially produced about 22 bhp. Later, the WR version was good for about 28 bhp. The

A 1929 poster advertises BMW's third Targa Floria win—a feat, reads the copy, that "bears testimony to the unequalled perfection of BMW motorcycles."

750cc R 63 also had a WR 750 sister. Carbureted versions of that racer produced about 40 bhp, while supercharged ones developed about 45 bhp.

The WR 750 had the blower mounted on top of the gearbox (first driven by the magneto shaft, later by a chain from the flywheel) that efficiently forced more of the fuel/air mixture into the nearby cylinders. Sepp Hopf experimented with Cozette centrifugal superchargers as well as Zoller, chain-driven, rotary-vane-type units. His supercharged racers—referred to as *Kompressors*—dominated German events in 1929, and Hans Soenius' '27, '28, and '29 German championships gave BMW six consecutive national titles.

Henne, meanwhile, had his eye on the world speed record then held by British riders Bert Le Vack and Oliver Baldwin, and on September 19, 1929, he rolled his short-stroke, supercharged 735cc works bike onto a country road north of Munich in an attempt to claim the record as his own. The machine had been designed by Schleicher prior to his departure from BMW but was prepared by Sepp Hopf, an excellent mechanic who had been saved from life as a shoemaker by Schleicher himself.

By 1932, Henne was setting world records so quickly that BMW's ad department could hardly keep up. This poster announced the addition of nine more (set at a Vienna one-kilometer sprint event), and gave the public a look at Henne's first experiments with streamlining.

Henne cut quite a figure that day, his racing outfit—white overalls, rubber-banded at the wrist to keep out the wind—complemented by a custom helmet that was similar in shape to those used by serious cyclists today. In 1930 Henne added a tail cone to the ensemble, which—like the helmet—was an attempt to bring some streamlining to the un-faired motorcycle. Despite the somewhat comical appearance, Henne's additions may have helped: his 134.78 mph mile was good for a new world record. Not content to let a record stand even when he himself was its owner, he went on to break his own record *six times* before the decade was finished, and his constant search for more and more speed had excellent results for BMW in terms of both publicity and retail sales.

The next decade began with a fierce back-and-forth battle between Henne and Joe Wright, who rode a Zenith motorcycle powered by a 1,000cc JAP V-twin engine. Wright took the record from Henne early in 1930 and Henne took it back in September of that year (with a top speed of 137.66 mph), only to have Wright register a blistering 150.73 mph in November 1931. It was a feat that Henne tried to match several times in the years following, only to see himself come up short and retail sales begin to fall. Henne was desperate for a break and eventually went straight to the top, convincing Popp to bring Rudolf Schleicher back into the BMW fold.

Schleicher was persuaded to return in 1931, and he quickly boosted Henne's power with the design of a multi-plate supercharger that allowed Henne to best Wright in November 1932 with a two-run average of 151.77 mph—a record that Henne himself (naturally) shattered two years later. By the time Henne was finished—though only with that particular motorcycle—the record stood at 159.10 mph.

In between record attempts, Henne was called to duty as part of the team sent to represent Germany at the 1933 ISDT in Wales. There were 143 entries that year, only three of them BMWs. Piloted by Henne, Stelzer, and Josef Mauermeyer, the three German machines scored a total of one silver and two golds, taking overall best at the annual competition. Although the foreign press was not inclined to say anything pleasant about the German government at the time—Adolph Hitler's rapid rise to absolute power was already setting

Although there's nothing not funny about a cone affixed to a man's hindquarters, Henne's speed was serious business. He was exceeding 150 mph at the time this photo was taken.

There's a reason that today's Tour de France riders wear helmets much like Henne's 1936 version for time trials: the science was sound.

off alarm bells throughout the rest of Europe—
they couldn't say anything but "well done" to all
three 750cc BMW riders, who lost but a single
mark between them. The following year, it was
Germany's turn to host the ISDT, and the BMW
riders again went home with gold.

BMW, like Germany itself, was beginning to
recover from the European Depression that had
seen 43 percent of the German labor force unem-
ployed in 1932. Although the political climate was
tumultuous at best and frightening at worst, the
economy was showing a positive, though sluggish,
response to forced spending, and German manufacturers were being encouraged more and more
vehemently to engage in competitive events. It
was into this world that BMW introduced one of
the most important machines in its history: the
500 Kompressor, a purpose-built Grand Prix racer.

The production models of the mid 1930s utilized a pressed steel frame, but the Kompressor returned to a lighter, tubular frame and featured a
host of new features and improvements. In direct
contrast to most of its competition (which typically
used high engine compression ratios and low
boost pressures), BMW's Zoller blower delivered a

*>BMW had plenty to show off by the time the
1930 Paris Salon rolled around, but Henne's 500cc
record-breaker sat front and center.*

boost of one atmosphere, allowing them to design motors with relatively low compression ratios. In addition to delivering up to 80 bhp, BMW's system used less fuel—an obvious advantage, particularly in longer races.

The Kompressor's design incorporated long induction ports that ran under the cylinders to the rear intakes to ensure superior cooling, and the crankcases and gearbox housing were cast from magnesium, resulting in a surprisingly light motorcycle at 302 lbs. To the new-to-BMW four-speed, foot-operated gearbox was added yet another first for the company: oil-filled telescopic front forks. Also designed by Schleicher, these forks soon showed up on ISDT works bikes, Henne's sidecars, and on the 1935 R 12 production machine—the first production motorcycle in the world to feature such technology. To offset the ground-clearance issues introduced by the flat-twin's protruding cylinders, the Grand Prix machines utilized a larger tire than production models did.

Despite the advancements, it was perhaps not immediately clear to the racing community what the dawn of the Kompressor would mean for the future; at its June 1935 debut, rider Ludwig Kraus

>*Henne wasn't breaking any speed records while negotiating Harz Run on this R 4 in 1933, but he was certainly helping to prove a thing or two about the brand's durability.*

This 1920 750cc supercharged racer was the first model to feature a Zoller blower that was installed transversely and driven by bevel gears. More power inevitably means more fuel consumption, hence the auxiliary fuel tank belted to the upper frame rails.

>An example of a 1935 500cc works bike. The supercharger is in the now-familiar position, in front of the motor; note the longer, smoother inlet tract. This particular motorcycle made its first outing at the Avus track, with Ludwig Kraus as pilot.

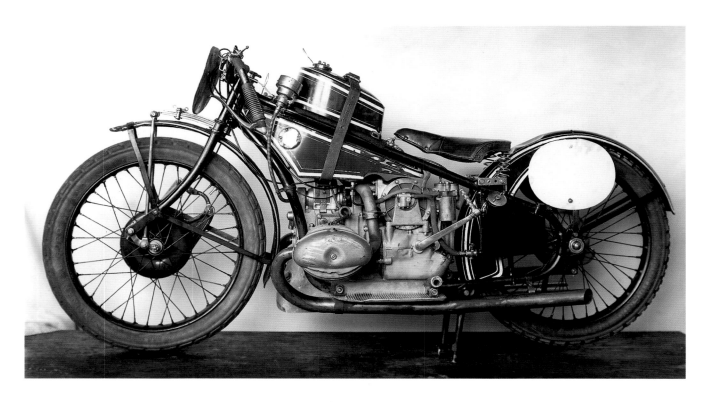

The 1935 ISDT team of (from left to right) Ludwig Kraus, Ernst Henne, and Josef Stelzer rode detuned Kompressors to a third consecutive event victory.

circled the banked Avus track at an average speed of 106 mph but was defeated by a Husqvarna. Respectable, certainly, but not enough to put any real fear into the competition. Later that year, the German ISDT team backed up their '33 and '34 performances by notching victory aboard detuned Kompressors, but it was not until the following year, 1936, that the Kompressor really set loose on the competition, both in the service of more Ernst Henne record-breaking attempts as well as on the Grand Prix circuit.

Long before the Grand Prix riders of the 1980s faced their powerful but brutally hard-to-ride 500cc machines, BMW riders Otto Ley and Karl Gall were doing their very best to hang on to their '36 works Kompressors—and it was no easy task. Ley, however, managed two second-place finishes before wrapping up the season with the Kompressor's historic first Grand Prix victory, at the August round in Sweden. It was enough to gain a measure of respect in the international community, but BMW felt itself capable of much more. Henne helped BMW to end the season on a high note by setting a new, 169.14 mph speed record aboard the first fully streamlined Kompressor (also

An inside look at the fully enclosed Kompressor that spelled the end of the infamous tailcone. In 1937, it helped Henne attain speeds in excess of 180 mph.

>Henne's world record-breaking attempts—like this November '37 one, taking place on the autobahn near Frankfurt—usually involved more than just the two people needed to push-start his 500cc machine. BMW executives and top-level government officials were all keenly interested in seeing the German brand impress.

Henne wasn't the only one making his mark on the world stage in 1937. Grand Prix riders like Otto Ley (77) and Karl Gall helped BMW to notch more GP victories than any other brand that year.

>Ley rails his 500cc supercharger around the Avus banking in practice. He would finish second to Gall at the German GP, but he had other victories ahead.

Henne's first 500cc record-breaker), whose aluminum shell completely enclosed both rider and motorcycle and even had its own tail fin, allowing Henne to retire his personal cone.

Schleicher and Henne, however, felt that Henne's Kompressor—like those contending in the GP circuit—was also capable of more. Henne's 169.14 mph result had in fact been the average of two passes: one that had been greatly affected by wind, and the other that had reached an astounding 180.20 mph. Six months later, Englishman Eric Fernihough broke Henne's record aboard a home-built Brough Superior, and Italian Piero Taruffi in turn took it from him via a 500cc Gilera. But Henne would have the last word—and a very, very long word it was. In November 1937, he posted a world speed record of 173.37 mph that stood for fourteen years.

It proved to be a season to remember for the Grand Prix riders, as well…. For some time, the Kompressor's lack of rear suspension had been something of an oddity among the fully sprung British machines, but when Ley and Gall arrived on the GP grid at the start of the '37 season, their machines were finally equipped with Alexander von Falkenhausen-designed plunger rear suspension. The BMWs were suddenly a true match for their British competition. That year also saw Englishman John Milns 'Jock' West—sales manager for J. Aldington, head of British BMW importers—join BMW's stable of racers, and the trio immediately began notching GP victories for the BMW brand, taking more wins than any other manufacturer that year as well as the majority of wins in the series itself. Gall took the Dutch TT (Tourist Trophy) and German Grand Prix (and the German championship), Ley won the Swedish TT, and West took the Ulster Grand Prix.

West's participation in the Ulster GP was actually preceded by several "tests" of sorts. After first demonstrating his riding skills for then team-manager Sepp Hopf in the practice session of a German national round, BMW agreed to back West in the '37 Isle of Man TT—the brand's debut appearance in the already legendary race—shipping a factory bike and mechanic over for the event. West had contended in the race four times before (in various classes, and for other manufacturers), but his job for BMW was simply to finish the event and make a good showing, not to go for the

This 1937 poster celebrates the 1-2 victory of Ley and Gall at the Swedish GP (a repeat of their '36 results) and carries the tagline, "Successful production models prove their reliability."

glory. After all, BMW's reputation and West's future with the company were both on the line—in front of a very large audience. West finished a remarkable sixth even after a fuel leak stopped him on the last lap, causing him to have to push his bike back to the pits for refueling. At the time his Kompressor had begun to slow, observers noted, West had been on the tail of eventual TT winner Freddie Frith.

Jock West's performance in the TT earned him backing for his home race, the Ulster Grand Prix, which at the time was run on the ultra-fast Clady circuit. Clady featured plenty of heavily cambered, narrow roads, but was most famous for its front straight—7.5 miles of rippling tarmac whose bumps would regularly heave bikes into the air. Add pouring rain to the scene of this 246-mile race, and one can imagine the grim determination it took for the former grass-tracker to be unstoppable that day. His win marked the first time a non-British motorcycle had won the premier class at Ulster.

Although West didn't collect the championships and world records that other BMW riders amassed, he played an important part in the

brand's international presence at the time. In England, particularly, the likeable West became the face of BMW abroad, showing up in English newspapers and advertisements, often photographed while perched jauntily aboard various BMW models. As tensions were forever escalating between the two governments, it could not always have been a comfortable position for him (and indeed, when war was finally declared a few years later, BMW had to pull strings to get West and his wife out of Germany on one of the last flights to leave); but for West—who rode without pay—it was all about the bikes. Known for his good humor as well as his passion for the sport, he once described an early TT crash simply as, "I arrived at Ballacraine [a sharp turn] on a wet road but without my bike." The 1938 and '39 TTs, however, would provide West with some even better stories.

West, who rode without pay for the entirety of his racing career, repeated his Ulster victory in 1938.

< Englishman Jock West was another important part of BMW's phenomenal 1937 season (and beyond). His victory at the Ulster GP marked the first time a non-British bike had won the premier class there.

4

War clouds loom

Paddock politics often loom large in modern racing, but in the late 1930s, international and national politics permeated nearly every aspect of life in Europe. Any competitive sport that was played on the world stage was of particular interest to a government that wanted to prove its superiority, and motorsports in particular—which involved judgement not only of an athlete, but of German engineering itself—couldn't escape this kind of interference. From the top level of government came a decree that a German should win the Isle of Mann TT, and thus it was that Otto Ley, who was nearing retirement, was replaced with up-and-coming rider Georg (Shorsch) Meier for the 1938 running of the IOM.

Meier had started with BMW just the previous year, acting as Henne's substitute at the ISDT after Henne himself fell ill. It was reasonable to expect him to do well in the event—always an avid

>*Georg "Shorsch" ("Ironman") Meier was an off-road expert when he started with BMW, but he was so unimpressed by his own early road-race results that he tried to quit the team, twice. BMW officials wisely talked him back onto the bike both times.*

motorcyclist, he'd grown up speeding down rough Bavarian roads and had quickly made a name for himself first as a member of the Bavarian Police's motorcycle team, and later as a rider for the German Army's team. Both teams regularly competed in 1000km enduro events, and Meier was so successful in this format (generally aboard the pressed-steel-framed R 4), that by the age of 25, he'd earned the nickname *Der Gusseiserne Schorsch,* or "Ironman Georg." Ironically, the infamous off-road event ended on a racetrack that year—a type of venue with which Ironman Georg had no experience.

The German and British teams had finished the sixth day neck-and-neck, and as a tie breaker, they reconvened at Donington to settle the matter via speed trial. (The venerable Donington circuit was brand-new in Meier's time.) Despite his lack of experience, Meier surprised everyone by winning the speed trial that day—a remarkable achievement, though it wasn't enough to earn victory for the German team. Race officials had decided to handicap the 500cc BMWs by a full lap in order to level the playing field for the British team's 350cc AJS and Nortons, and in the end, Germany lost the

A former member of the Bavarian Police and German Army enduro teams, Meier (at right) was first hired as an ISDT replacement after Henne fell ill. When the off-road event adjourned to Donington racetrack to settle a tie, Meier—who had no road race experience—shocked everyone by winning the speed trial.

overall event by ten seconds. Germany's team managers, however, lost little time in recommending the army sergeant to the BMW factory squad.

Like West, Meier's first test for the company involved taking part in the practice session of a national round aboard one of BMW's 500cc flat-twin works bikes. According to a feature in *Classic Racer* magazine, Meier had completed only a few laps before he pulled off the track and announced that road racing was "far too dangerous" for his tastes. The BMW staff present actually had to persuade Meier to go back out again, but once he did so, he set the fourth-fastest time of the session.

Meier himself wasn't impressed by his own performance, though, nor was he satisfied with his fourth-place finish at Hockenheim a few weeks later in what was his first road race of any kind. With Meier determined to walk away from what he felt were mediocre results, BMW once again had to talk him back out onto the track. When Meier returned to asphalt for his second national race in early 1938, he finished ahead of teammate Karl Gall and at last began to think that perhaps he had some talent on a road race bike after all.

Meier, in fact, had the kind of natural ability

Karl Gall (shown here following a win at the '38 International Hamburg City Park race) was a talented rider who also served as a measuring stick for the upcoming Meier. Not until he could beat Gall did Meier think he might have a future on asphalt.

that made veteran racers from throughout Europe shake their heads in awe and envy. It became clear early in the '38 season that Meier, despite his rookie status, was a threat for both the German national and 500cc European championships, though he was still somewhat of an unknown when he appeared at the '38 Isle of Man TT with BMW teammates Gall and West. Meier had, at that point, only three road races under his belt, and he was facing a course that even today is considered perhaps the most dangerous ribbon to race.

Precisely because it is so arduous, the Isle of Man proves anticlimactic for competitors nearly as often as it is dangerous, and such was the case in BMW's '38 running of the TT. The team's works Kompressors featured larger brakes and 55 bhp at 7,000 rpm, none of which is helpful if you can't remove your warm-up spark plugs in time to get the race plugs in. Such was Meier's fate at the start line thanks to some stripped threads, and he was consigned to the grandstands for the rest of the race, a spectator at his very first TT. Gall had suffered a terrible crash in the previous day's practice—he ended up unconscious and face down in a stream, and would have drowned had Meier not

been just a few seconds behind him—which left West to carry the BMW flag alone. He finished fifth behind one of the factory Nortons.

Though a tough pill to swallow at the time, Meier later reflected that the DNS (did not start) had perhaps been a blessing in disguise considering his then lack of experience. Regardless, Georg didn't need to wait long for redemption: only fourteen days later he took victory at the Belgian Grand Prix, a stunning achievement for a 28-year-old off-road racer in only his fourth race on tarmac. Those tempted to think his victory was a fluke were soon silenced by a string of podiums for Meier and his unstoppable Kompressor; Meier took wins in Holland, Italy, and Germany on his way to being crowned 500cc European champion (and German National Champion) in his novice year.

Meanwhile, 1937 and '38 had likewise been exciting years for privateer BMW riders, who had been on the scene since the introduction of the R 37 but left to their own devices—or rather, left to the company's pressed-steel-frame production models—when BMW began developing works bikes (*Werksrennmaschinen*) for their factory riders. By 1936, BMW was established enough in the

Meier's '38 Isle of Man TT race was over almost before it began, but since he was then in his rookie road-race season, Meier later speculated that being sidelined that year was probably somewhat fortunate. The TT, after all, isn't known for tolerating inexperience.

Although disappointed with his TT showing, Meier won the Belgian Grand Prix only 14 days later—in the fourth road race of his career.

racing world to begin to give some serious thought to supporting the development of young German riders, and the following year saw the debut of the company's first true production racer: the R 5 SS (Super Sport). It was based, as the name implied, on the production 494cc R 5 ohv machine (which in turn drew heavily on the Kompressor), but with an increased power output that let privateers join factory riders in reaching 100 mph speeds on the track. The R 5 SS's modifications went beyond jetting and compression ratio changes, however (and far beyond the absence of a muffler and running lights); its chassis now included a tubular, arc-welded frame and oil-damped telescopic front forks, with levers and other controls set up to accommodate a low-profile, more-aggressive riding position.

The 1938 R 51 SS wasn't significantly different from its predecessor except in the plunger rear suspension it borrowed from that year's R 51 production model, but 1939 saw another leap forward in the form of BMW's first Rennsport—the R 51 RS—which incorporated the tank, seat, and larger wheels of the works bikes, featured spur gear-driven double cams, and added yet another

Meier ended his '38 rookie season with nothing less than the 500cc European championship. One imagines the veteran GP racers—as well as the other manufacturers—shaking their heads in dismay. BMW-loyal and younger than most of the riders on the grid, Meier was clearly just getting started.

The R 51 SS production racer was based on the production R5 ohv machine, which was already being modified and fielded by many privateers. Here, Hungarian motorcycle champion Endre Kozma lines up his modified R5 for a sprint race.

The 1939 R 51 RS (BMW's first Rennsport) built on the already-impressive R 51 SS, incorporated several features that had previously only been found on works bikes. The results added another 15 mph to available top speed.

15 mph of speed to previous models' 100 mph capabilities. But all three production racers were manufactured in such limited numbers that only select privateers actually contended the machines, and though the direct descendents of these bikes would be the next motorcycle to make BMW history, they aren't what 1939 is remembered for.

Even before crowds gathered around the *SS Fenella* to watch the 1939 BMW works bikes being unloaded, the Brits were worried. A no-name the year before, Meier returned as what was essentially world champion, and the Kompressor was by now well-developed and faster than ever. *The Motor Cycle's* regular reports on TT activity soon noted the Kompressor's remarkable drive out of corners, and journalists estimated that it had a solid 10 mph over the competition's flat speed.

If ever there was a pilot equal to his machine, it was Meier, who soon began to turn consistent 25-minute practice laps on the 37.73-mile circuit. But into this promising start came tragedy: Karl Gall—whose '38 TT crash had fractured his skull and broken his arm—crashed again in practice and fractured his skull a second time. The injury proved too much to recover from, and Gall passed away

By the time the Senior TT rolled around again, Georg Meier (center) was ready. He was joined at the historic '39 event by Jock West (left) and Karl Gall, but only two men would return home. Gall crashed in practice, fracturing his skull, and did not live out the week.

BMW considered withdrawing its entries following Gall's death, but in the end it was decided to press on. Here, Meier's type 255 machine is inspected prior to the start.

three days before the race went off. Fatal racing accidents weren't at all unheard of at the time, but it was enough to make senior BMW officials nearly withdraw their remaining entries. In the end, though, it was decided to stay put on the Isle and contend the race.

Meier was, if possible, more determined than ever when he left the start line sixteen minutes behind Harold Daniell, the previous year's race winner. Meier began to make up time so quickly that by the end of the first lap, he'd not only passed the race leader, but left teammate Jock West—who was vying for second with Velocette's Stanley Woods—52 seconds behind. His advantage continued to build, and despite a near-crash and a last-lap pit stop, Meier crossed the finish line two minutes and twenty seconds ahead of second-place finisher West. The post-race inspection of the winning motorcycle left its examiners in awe, and the resulting official ACU report made use of the adjectives "perfect" and "cool and clean" to describe the internals. The German company's 1-2 victory turned Isle of Man history on its ear and was everything the team and the company could have hoped for, as well as a fitting tribute to Gall.

Meier won the Dutch TT the following month and the Belgian Grand Prix a few weeks later, putting himself in the lead for a second European championship. Though Meier crashed at the August Swedish GP and injured his back seriously enough to end his season, it was a glorious time for BMW: the brand and its riders combined to form one of the most dominant and respected forces in racing, they owned the two most prestigious titles in sport, and it was all happening in front of crowds so large they'd look respectable even at a modern MotoGP event. It was a Golden Age, without question, and a stunning achievement for a company that had been forced to reinvent itself less than two decades before. Then into the dream marched yet another World War.

Knowing that industrial plants and Munich itself would be heavily bombed, BMW moved all of its works bikes from Munich to the small town of Berg on Lake Starnberg to wait out the conflict … except one. In Allach, another small town outside Munich, Georg Meier rolled his TT-winning machine into a hay barn and concealed it carefully, then pulled the doors shut behind him for what would turn out to be six long years.

Meier dominated the '39 TT aboard his supercharged BMW, running away with the Senior victory and crossing the finish line two minutes and twenty seconds ahead of the second-place finisher.

With a shield for each Senior winner, the TT's famous trophy has several more tiers on it these days. In 1939, however, organizers were surprised to be adding a German to all those English names.

< Surviving the TT is reason to rejoice, but winning it is something else entirely. Jock West (at right, shaking hands with Meier), too, had reason to celebrate: he'd just finished second to Meier.

BMW's first golden era of motorcycle racing ended, quite literally, in flames. With the beginning of WWII, BMW was facing six years of heavy bombing.

61

Rebuilding after the war

In what must have felt like the worst kind of deja vu, BMW post-World War II found itself in much the same position WWI had left it. With Germany once again a defeated power and subject to the rules of the Allied Control Commission, the company was prohibited from making motorcycles and spent the next few years eking out an existence via the manufacture of agricultural equipment, bicycles, pots and pans, and other miscellaneous items.

BMW hardly looked lucky at this point—bombing had razed approximately one-third of its Munich plants and much of the equipment that survived was seized and shipped out-of-country by the Allies. The Russians had actually started copying the R 71 motorcycle even before the war, and now tooling, patents, and parts were also taken by France as "war reparations" and given to the CMR company. (Later, CMR became Ratier, which made

>Production building 10, one of BMW's original production sites, was (not surprisingly) destroyed by air raids. Somewhere in the background is the house where Max Friz designed the R 32.

elegant flat twins of its own design from the mid-'50s to the mid-'60s and nearly became a real rival of BMW's.)

It had taken, however, a degree of luck (and diplomacy) to make it even that far, as BMW had first narrowly avoided seeing all of its assets destroyed in Hitler's "scorched earth" campaign and then barely avoided having two of its surviving factories leveled by the Allies. By the dawn of 1946, BMW was a far different company from the one that had closed out 1939, but help came from an unexpected source: the now-defunct Third Reich. When the Allies released confiscated assets in 1948, BMW found itself the beneficiary of 63.5 million marks—money owed to them by the previous regime for the purchase of military motorcycles and sidecars.

With that influx of cash and the restrictions on motor vehicle manufacturing now somewhat relaxed, BMW was able to return to the two-wheel market. Although they were initially only allowed to make a limited number of single-cylinder machines, an updated version of the R 51 became available by 1950, and precisely because the company had been ahead of the industry when the

Much as it had been after WWI, BMW was subject to the conquering power. From 1945 through '46, Allied Confiscation Commission members were a regular sight at the Munich plant.

< With the end of the conflict, it was time to take stock of what remained. On this 1945 model drawing of the BMW Munich-Milbertshofen plant, bomb damage is marked in red.

The R 71, a legendarily robust military machine,
was being copied by the Russians even before WWII
started. (The Russians had acquired an R 71 to copy
through a Scandinavian intermediary—a bit of
subterfuge that was retroactively made "legal"
under the provisions of the Molotov-Ribbentrop
Treaty of 1939.) The U.S. Army also noted the
advantages of this model and sent captured R 71s
back to the United States, where they were copied
by both Harley-Davidson and Indian.

>Once permitted to begin manufacturing
motorcycles again, R 51s became the backbone
of BMW's retail offerings.

war broke out, the R 51/2 was still modern enough to be well received by the buying public.

Unfortunately for BMW, after World War II, changes to FIM rules banned the famous "Kompressors" from international competition. German riders and teams were not welcomed back to Grands Prix racing until 1950. Race fans, however, hadn't had to wait quite that long to see BMWs (even supercharged models, which remained legal in German domestic competition) back in action. It turned out that Georg Meier wasn't the only one who'd carefully hidden a beloved Kompressor, as around the country, as well as in other European nations, pre-WWII BMW race bikes began emerging from various hiding places almost as soon as the war was over, having been protected by amateur racers and motorcycle enthusiasts alike who couldn't bear to see such beautiful machines become casualties of war.

Anyone spectating at a German motorcycle race in 1946 would have witnessed a busy and exciting race scene that almost exactly mirrored the national series of 1939. In many cases, it was quite literally the same riders on the same bikes. Even the podiums looked familiar, as Meier teamed up

with Ludwig Kraus to form the Veritas squad and
was soon collecting countless victories at the great
German circuits of the day—Hackenheim, Solitude, Schotten—while engaging arch-rivals like
NSU's Heiner Fleischmann in fierce battles. The
battles usually ended with Meier on top, and he
collected four consecutive national championships
beginning in 1947, adding a fifth (his sixth total) in
1953. The early '50s also saw the rise of a young
rider who, together with Henne and Meier, would
complete what is perhaps the company's most
memorable trifecta of riders to date.

Seventeen years Meier's junior and a lifelong
motorcycle enthusiast, Walter Zeller grew up idol-
izing the older rider. Even as an 18-year-old novice
racer, Zeller imagined himself lining up against
Meier, but when the two did take to the track together the year after that, it was as teammates.
Meier in fact became Zeller's mentor, and Zeller
was unwavering in his admiration for and grati-
tude toward the man who taught him the intrica-
cies of speed for the next three years, and whom
he felt contributed greatly to his own 1951 German national championship, won at the age of 20.

German race bikes, regardless of brand, were

*It was inevitable that Meier would eventually take
a back seat to Zeller; here, he does so literally. Zeller
won the 500cc class at Norisring and stopped to take
his mentor, Meier, along for a victory lap. Meier
himself won the Supercharged class that day
(the Kompressors were still legal in German
domestic racing).*

*< Meier became famous as a road racer, but the
former motorcycle cop was initially an off-road
specialist. He's seen here aboard an R 51/3, returning
to his roots in a 1953 enduro. The bike is fitted
with an oversized front wheel, high-mount exhausts,
and a duplicate cable set.*

still a ferociously supercharged pack when BMW was reaccepted into the FIM community in 1950. When the time came to return to the world championship in 1951, however, BMW debuted a new flat-twin, race-specific, twin-cylinder engine designed by Leonard Ischinger.

It was with an M255-powered machine that Zeller had won the German championship, but it was quite obviously not enough to make BMW a contender in international competition. In doing away with the blower, these naturally aspirated dohc twins had said goodbye to more than 30 bhp, and most of the other manufacturers were now using swing-arm technology that was far superior to BMWs pre-war-era plunger rear suspension. The disadvantages were too significant to be denied, and instead of floundering through a potentially exasperating and embarrassing year, BMW decided to sit out the 1952 Grand Prix season. The official company line regarding this decision was that they wanted to focus on dominating that year's ISDT, but they were in fact using that time to secretly develop the second generation of 500cc Grand Prix racer.

Because the company was interested in increasing the presence of German BMW riders on the world stage, the decision was made to focus on the creation of a competitive but affordable production race machine. After several variations were rapidly tried and discarded, the new model was introduced to the public at the Frankfurt Show in late 1953 as the RS54 Rennsport.

BMW had successfully kept the development of the new motorcycle a relative secret, making the Rennsport something of a surprise when it was unveiled. It was announced that only between thirty and fifty of the motorcycles would be produced; this was due to the incredible expense of manufacturing the Rennsports, which were built by the same highly skilled crew responsible for the works machines, and to the same standards. In fact, aside from variations in the bore and stroke numbers—and the fact that the production racer used carburetors where the works bikes used fuel injection—they were virtually the same machine.

Although the Rennsport's dohc horizontal twin-cylinder engine was by now very familiar, BMW engineering chief Alex von Falkenhausen had updated it significantly—with a pair of Fisher-Amal 30mm carburetors, it produced 45 bhp at

It's no surprise to see Georg Meier (far left) heading off to the 1952 International Six Day Trial with the works team. What's somewhat less well known is that Walter Zeller (second from left) was also an accomplished off-road racer.

8,000 rpm—and the machine itself featured a number of other refinements. An all-indirect gearbox offered a choice of five or four ratios (allowing the rider to fit the machine to the venue), a swingarm replaced the now-antiquated plunger rear suspension (with the driveshaft encased in the right "arm"), and although the Rennsport had made its debut wearing telescopic forks, those production models that rolled out of the workshop sported Earles-type front forks that engineers felt better assisted braking under high speeds.

During this period, the factory BMWs lacked top speed and raw horsepower as compared to the multis. In order to be competitive over the season, the German bikes needed to out-handle the Italian jobs; they needed to be more reliable and to eke all the speed they could out of the twin-cylinder design.

On the handling front, BMW was among the first manufacturers to equip their motorcycles with hydraulic steering dampers and hydraulically actuated brakes. Reliability came at the expense of careful building and lavishing the best possible materials on both the full-works bikes and the couple of dozen Rennsports sold to privateers. The

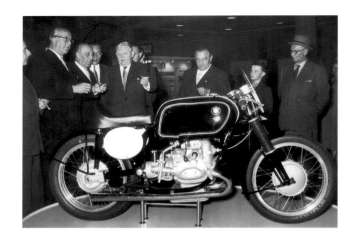

Top-level BMW staff gather at the launch of the RS54 Rennsport. Third from right is Helmut Werner Bönsch, the company's director of planning. Fourth from right is Ludwig Erhard, one of the principal bureaucrats in charge of Germany's postwar economic reconstruction.

>People were eager for entertainment in the post-WWII era. This 1951 round of the German motorcycle championship was held on a former Zeppelin Airfield in Nuremberg, in front of a crowd totalling almost 100,000.

superior cooling offered by the boxer design made its contribution to the finishing percentage, too.

Considering BMW's many land speed records and its extensive aviation experience, it's not surprising that the company was very proficient in streamlining. The "dustbin" fairings of the mid-'50s also helped make the German bikes more competitive, and this was particularly true on the Isle of Man TT course, which—as it traverses a mountain pass—has always been subject to strong winds. During the 1957 TT, Zeller rode with and without the fairing, depending on wind conditions (the dustbins were severely affected by crosswinds), and he found that the fairing increased top speed by well over 30 miles an hour! This advantage, too, was lost to BMW when the FIM banned full fairings in 1958.

Only twenty-four or twenty-five Rennsports were produced as solo racers (they were so expensive to make that there was virtually no profit in them for the company), but several more found glory in sidecar racing, a genre in which the engine's low, horizontal layout was a true advantage, actually facilitating drift, with the shaft drive likewise a sudden blessing. While engineers

struggled to improve Zeller's works bike throughout the next several years (Zeller took some incredible victories on his way to the German championship but could not impress on the world stage),
Wilhelm Noll and Fritz Cron—now in an impressively streamlined sidecar—handily won the 1954
Sidecar World Championship.

Fuel injection had been the focus of much development since the introduction of the M253 production series; by 1955 the works bikes were

This photo, taken at Hockenheim in 1954, illustrates the similarities between the Rennsport production racer (#25, Robert Zeller) and the factory racer (#21, Walter Zeller). Only the carburetors on the Rennsport give it away. The other machines on the front row are an MV Agusta (#32, Nello Pagani) and a Moto Guzzi (#26, Ken Kavanagh).

>The BMW racing department was busy in the early '50s, not just with the team's current solo and sidecar racers, but with the development of the RS54 Rennsport.

Walter Zeller took third place on a BMW in the 500cc class as an amateur rider. The full fairing shown here on Walter Zeller's '57 German GP bike was in its swan song; the FIM banned them the following year.

>In this 1954 photo, Zeller's works machine is fitted with Bosch fuel injection …

>… but obviously not all 253s were fitted with fuel injection all the time; this one has carburetors.

alternating between fuel injection and Dell'Orto carburetors (depending on venue). BMW made a full-time return to the 500cc world championship for the 1956 season, and although Zeller did not win a championship event that year, he was consistent enough to finish second to the legendary John Surtees, which—as history proves—was no mean feat.

Surtees, one of the most talented racers of the day (and still the only man to be world champion on both two wheels and four) tried his hand on one of the works bikes in 1955, at the Nurburgring. He did not finish the race due to mechanical problems, but was impressed by the machine and later said that he felt he could have won the championship on it the following year. When BMW's board of directors took too long to offer him a contract, however, he signed with MV Agusta. In '56, Surtees won the championship for the Italian marque. That may have been as close as the German company ever came to winning the blue-riband class in the new world championship.

After failing to put Surtees under contract, BMW hired the very experienced Scot, Fergus Anderson. Although he was old (for a motorcycle racer) he was still plenty fast; he'd won world championships for Moto Guzzi in '53 and '54. Anderson didn't get much further than Surtees, and came to a worse end. He crashed fatally in Belgium after just a few races, at a time when it seemed as though he'd really adapted to the boxer. BMW's solo racers continued to post respectable results: Ernest Hiller took second at the opening round of the 1957 season, and privateer Gerald Klinger bested Zeller himself in Austria one week later. Zeller earned third at the world championship opener shortly after, then shook off a disappointing TT finish (he retired from third position due to a mechanical) but took yet another third at the second championship round, followed in fifth by Hiller.

Throughout the '50s, the Italian works racers produced by MV Agusta, Gilera, and Moto Guzzi were very complex and expensive. MV was really a profitable aircraft company that raced motorcycles as Count Domenico Agusta's personal hobby; cost was no object. But Gilera and Moto Guzzi were gradually bankrupting themselves in the effort to win championships. In 1958, both firms withdrew from the world championship. BMW had always

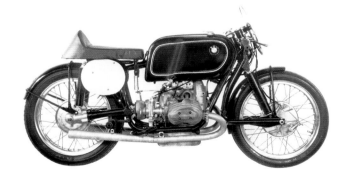

been a little more parsimonious, so the company could afford to stay in the game for a few more years, but it, too, faced financial difficulties and gradually wound down its 500cc-class involvement. Although the results had been (and continued to be) impressive in relative terms, second places didn't have much marketing impact. With Zeller forced to retire in 1958 due to family obligations, the '59 season looked a bit bleak for BMW fans, though Hiller and another privateer named Dickie Dale provided an excellent excuse to cheer, as the two put on a string of superb rides in the national series as well as several world championship rounds, Dale in fact earning third overall in the 500cc world series. They were a strange contrast to multi-world championship winner Geoff Duke's '58 performance. Though signed to contend all international events, the talented rider—who'd watched Georg Meier fly by in the TT as a child—experienced a string of bad luck (and difficulty adapting to the BMW) that saw him lose factory support before the year was over. Fumio Ito was the last rider to field an RS in world championship competition, its swan song coming in 1960.

Zeller's retirement marked the end of an era for BMW's racing history, and he didn't leave empty-handed. BMW officials presented Zeller with this 600cc supercharged motorcycle—the only supercharged BMW ever licensed for road use. It was created from a sidecar racing engine and an RS54 frame with telescopic forks.

< Dickie Dale on the Isle of Man with the Type 253 works racing motorcycle complete with fairing.

A little (actually, quite a lot) on the side

BMW riders were hampered by the lack of full fairings and superchargers, but those weren't the only technological challenges they faced. Tires, frames, and suspensions were all improving (the first "Manx" Nortons with Featherbed frames were built by the McAndless brothers in 1950; rear swingarms became standard equipment in that decade; and hydraulic suspension units had benefited from wartime aircraft R&D). With those improvements came increased corner speeds and lean angles, which meant that the BMW boxer twins—with their wide, protruding cylinders and reduced cornering clearance—faced an inherent limitation in the highest levels of competitive riding. Fortunately for BMW, the 1950s also ushered in the perfect platform for the company's robust boxer motors: sidecar racing.

The wide BMW motor was no disadvantage in a sidecar, since the vehicles didn't lean into the

>Although this shot of a restored Rennsport proves that it can be leaned impressively, by the mid-'50s motorcycle handling had improved to the point that the boxer design's protruding cylinders were becoming a worry. From this point on, race tuners developed a variety of tricks to increase cornering clearance, from lifting engines slightly to shortening pistons and con rods, to chamfering valve covers. Of course, none of those techniques were needed in sidecar racing!

By the mid-'50s, BMW was rapidly evolving the works sidecar outfits. This picture, taken in 1954 on the Solitude circuit, shows Noll & Cron in a rather ungainly-looking streamlined outfit ahead of Schneider & Strauss on their private entry.

>Alexander von Falkenhausen had a huge impact on the development of BMW motorcycles, especially for front and rear suspension. But later in the 1960s he was BMW's car engine mastermind; for example, he designed the fabulous engine of the BMW 2002 Cult car. In this photo from the 1940s, Falkenhausen is seated in a race car of his own design.

turns. In fact, the motor's low center of gravity gave it a real advantage, and the shaft drive (which in those pre-Paralever days was something of a disadvantage on a solo machine) also worked exceptionally well on a sidecar rig. The relatively low-tech twin-cylinder design had always offered better low and mid-range torque than rival four-cylinder motors, yet superior top-end power compared to the Norton single-cylinder motors used to win the sidecar title in the years 1949 to '53.

Those first years of the Sidecar World Championship had been dominated by Eric Oliver, who drove a Norton motorcycle with a Watsonian sidecar. In 1954, Oliver's luck ran out. He was injured after starting the season strongly, and in that moment of weakness, the BMW team of Wilhelm Noll (driver) and Fritz Cron (passenger) pounced. They won the final three races of the season, and the title.

Indeed, they began one of the longest periods of domination in the history of racing. From 1954 to 1974, BMW won the sidecar class in the world championship on no less than 19 occasions. BMW-powered rigs were also favored by privateers and dominated the national series. Since the company's road-going motorcycles were often equipped with "chairs," sidecar racing served a useful commercial purpose, too.

Many of the Rennsport production racers soon found themselves sprouting third wheels. Their development took place largely under the watchful eye of Falkenhausen, himself a winning BMW competitor both on motorcycles and in automobiles. After earning three gold medals at the ISDT, he went on to claim more than a hundred victories in BMW 315 and 358 cars, and even took some time off to found his own company (which manufactured sports cars as well as race-specific autos). He returned to BMW in time to head up Wilhelm Noll and Fritz Cron's 1955 speed-record-setting sidecar effort—which logged 174.12 mph and broke no less than eighteen world records—and simply never slowed down.

In the early '50s, racing sidecar rigs were fairly conventional racing motorcycles attached to a low platform for the passenger. The "passenger," in this case, wasn't sitting in the sidecar, but was rather a very active participant in the driving process. The passenger moved around and hung off the sidecar dramatically, shifting his weight both

from side to side in the turns, as well as fore and aft for maximum traction under braking and acceleration.

Noll and Cron's success had begun simply: a Steib sidecar was attached to a RS54 solo machine, creating a unit that was immediately, thrillingly competitive. At the time BMW made its real debut on the sidecar-racing scene, the results were almost completed dominated by British racers. Cyril Smith was well known internationally, while fellow Norton driver Oliver was perhaps the most prominent. Oliver had won the 1954 Isle of Man TT's sidecar class—the first time sidecars were included in the TT since being dropped from the event in 1926—and was an innovative designer as well. He was the first racer to move the third wheel forward (most ordinary sidecars placed the third wheel abreast of the motorcycle's rear wheel), and he'd given the world its first look at a "kneeler" sidecar at the previous year's Belgian Grand Prix.

Kneelers represented a mammoth step forward in the evolution of the sidecar. Drivers who had previously sat on their motorcycles were now quite literally on their knees, lowering the center

>*By the middle of the season, Noll was driving a fully enclosed outfit …*

>*… seen here in full flight at Monza. At the time, the circuit was one of the fastest in the world, so the added streamlining would certainly have had an impact on lap times.*

of gravity and thus hugely improving their machines' cornering capabilities.

BMW didn't pioneer the kneeler and did not, in fact, adopt the chassis technology until 1958. (Even then, it was a matter of taste; Max Deubel won championships well into the 1960s on a fairly conventional "sitter.") But in some ways, the development turned out to favor BMW's engine configuration more than it did the original Norton. The venerable British single had not only a huge vertical cylinder, but it sported an even larger cylinder head and cambox on top, thus limiting how low the driver could position his own weight. BMW's layout, in this instance, was a real "lay out," since the driver's chest could sit little more than a foot above the track surface.

Full streamlining had remained legal in the sidecar class, and fairings developed quickly—Noll's machine started the '54 world championship season naked, and finished it fully enclosed in an aluminum shell. In fact, most changes made to BMW sidecars post-1953 fell under the category of chassis improvements: wheels and tires became smaller but wider; drum brakes evolved into hydraulically operated drum brakes, then discs; and

In the mid-'50s, the sporting R 69 was fitted with an Earles fork. Ernest Earles' patent was for a leading link pivoting behind the wheel. It reduced fork dive under braking—a holy grail still pursued with the Telelever and Duolever designs used on most contemporary R and K models.

what was once a two-part gas tank set low on the bike was soon rejoined and moved to the sidecar itself. And although the Earles-type fork used in the RS had such high steering inertia that it adversely affected BMW solo racers, they proved to be yet another example of a serendipitous match for the BMW sidecars.

When the 1954 sidecar season began, the BMW team faced, in Oliver, a four-time world champion who had come to seem virtually invincible, and who'd handily won the first three rounds of the '54 season. It was Oliver himself, however, who proved fallible, breaking his arm in an off-track excursion just prior to the German round of the series. With Oliver out of the picture at the German GP, the success of BMW's works team there—featuring the pairs of Noll/Cron and Walter Schneider/Hans Strauss—lacked some of the impact it might have otherwise. But when Oliver returned for the following round, Noll and Cron quickly made up for it, tying him for a total of three victories each and then taking the world championship thanks to their superior finishes in the early rounds of the season. Though Norton and other British manufacturers didn't know it at

Noll & Cron parade their world championship-winning sidecar outfit through Munich to the BMW factory, in what would be the first of many such celebrations. Unfortunately, there would be more than a few funerals, as well, since sidecar racing proved at least as dangerous as solo racing.

the time, their long-time dominance of the three-wheeled world had just come to an abrupt end.

Motorcycles had always had a thrilling allure, but sidecars, at least commercially, had a much more staid appeal: They were family transportation for the working man. In fact, there was a time when the sidecar industry actively discouraged the sport, as sidecar makers thought the image of sidecar "monkeys" hanging inches above the road would scare regular passengers.

Indeed, sidecar racing was every bit as thrilling—and risky—as it looked. In one sense, it was even more dangerous than racing solos, since every crash involved at least two people. Perusing the various BMW champions during that famous 21-season run, it's impossible to gloss over the number of times that the injury or death of an incumbent represented an opportunity for the next would-be heir to the sidecar throne.

The BMW sidecar stable was bursting at the seams in the late '50s. In addition to Noll/Cron and Schneider/Strauss, the company was represented on track by the teams of Fritz Hillebrand/Manfred Grunwald and Willi Faust/Karl Remmert, both of which would play a large part in the creation of

BMW's sidecar legacy by virtue of their success and, unfortunately, attendant tragedy.

The 1955 season belonged to Faust and Remmert; the duo took victories at three of the six world championship rounds and brought home the title. Later that same year, however, Faust was injured and Remmert was killed in a practice-session crash at Hockenheim, and although Faust eventually recovered, he did not return to racing.

Hillebrand and Grunwald found success particularly on the Isle of Man, contending the '54, '56, and '57 TT sidecar races on the Clypse Course. In only their debut outing, the pair notched a second-place finish behind Oliver (who drove with passenger Les Nutt). When they returned to the Isle in '56, they came out on top of a three-way battle for the lead with drivers Schneider and Noll, and in '57 they were truly transcendent, breaking race records, lap records, and the will of their opponents as they took the TT victory on their way to becoming that season's world champions. Hillebrand, however, would never hold the trophy. The duo had already established an untouchable points lead in the championship when a crash at the

From left to right: Noll, Faust, Remmert, and Cron, at Solitude in 1955. Faust & Remmert were world champions that year, but Remmert did not live to enjoy it. He was killed that very season at Hockenheim.

< Despite the extreme nature of sidecar racing, BMW simultaneously promoted sidecars as utilitarian vehicles appropriate for even the most staid, practical-minded customers.

Bilbao circuit claimed his life. Grunwald chose to retire soon after.

Noll and Cron had previously claimed their second world championship in 1956, after which Noll also opted for retirement. With Noll in retirement and two other brilliant pairings lost to tragedy, the torch was passed to Schneider and Strauss for 1958. The duo had finished second in the previous year's championship, but the promotion to being BMW's sole factory sidecar team was not necessarily a step up. Motorcycle sales had been plunging since the mid-'50s as cars became more affordable, and motorcycle manufacturers had dropped into bankruptcy one by one. BMW, as always, was a survivor, and although race results were still an important aspect of retail sales, it was decided that the company could not support more than one sidecar effort. (Motorcycle development, too, had essentially ground to a halt post-1955, due in large part to the amount of resources being devoted to a series of expensive eight-cylinder cars.)

Despite the suddenly minimalist corporate climate, Schneider and Strauss might have expected to run rampant over the rest of the field during

By the time Schneider & Strauss retired at the end of the '59 season, BMW had won six consecutive championships. That was plenty of reason to print yet another poster.

>BMW was quick to use its sidecar-racing success in advertising, and its cadre of racers kept the ink flowing.

the upcoming season were it not for a handful of non-factory BMW racers who set out to make them work for it. The Swiss duo of Florion Camathias and Hilmer Cecco put their privateer Rennsport in the way of the factory boys every chance they got, and the soon-to-be-infamous Helmut Fath likewise made the '58 season a difficult one for the company team. Schneider and Strauss took the title in both '58 and '59, however, after which Schneider followed Noll into retirement.

From there, all eyes turned to Camathias and Cecco, but infighting led Cecco to change horses, joining a rival driver. That left Camathias flailing, and he picked up a passenger with whom he never quite gelled. Still, such was BMW's dominance in the world of sidecar racing that despite the rampant attrition, the German company retained not only the world title, but took home each of the top three positions, second and third filled by drivers Fritz Scheidegger and Pip Harris.

Harris, a privateer, had experienced some success already in the Sidecar World Championship, finishing third in 1956 aboard a Norton and making several good runs at individual Grand Prix. In

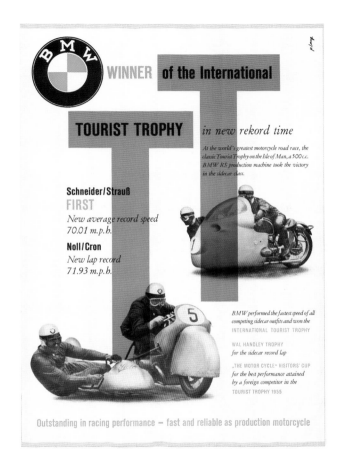

1958 he bought a second-hand Rennsport (splitting the cost of the machine with a fellow racer), and although adapting to the bike took some time, he won the Dutch round of the 1960 series and was an important complement to the factory riders.

The 1960 world champions, privateers Fath and passenger Alfred Wohlgemuth, began the '61 season by lapping the entire field at the first round, but in poor conditions at Nurburgring—the track was wet, and visibility low—the pair crashed, and Wohlgemuth was killed. Anyone who's spent time around sidecar racers knows that the relationship between driver and passenger is typically very close (they often finish each other's sentences like an old married couple). It is no surprise, then, that Fath could not bring himself to return to racing for five long years.

Camathias and Cecco made up in time for the '61 season, but tragedy—which never stayed away from racetracks for long in those days—struck yet again, as Cecco succumbed to fatal injuries following an early-season crash at the Italian round of the championship. The factory's eyes fell upon Max Deubel and passenger Emil Horner, and what support BMW had to give was put behind the German pair. They responded by taking the next four consecutive world championships.

The Deubel/Horner partnership—on their traditional, "sitter" outfit—was the most successful one seen in years; it held off the efforts of BMW-mounted Scheidegger and Camathias, while racking up so many victories that a non-win evoked more comment that did a triumph. Once Scheidegger teamed up with new passenger John Robinson, however, the decorated German team experienced two seasons of intense competition, finishing second to the Swiss/British pair each year.

The two pairs were fierce rivals, and put on particularly good shows on the Isle of Man. In 1965, it was the Germans who won the Sidecar TT, breaking the lap record in their quest to outpace the other BMW machine. In 1966, it was Scheidegger and Robinson who grabbed victory— by a margin of only four-fifths of a second. Not long afterward, the duo was stripped of their TT win by the FIM for an alleged fuel irregularity, but Scheidegger appealed the decision twice and the victory was eventually handed back.

Scheidegger, a former grass tracker (as a

Helmut Fath's creativity as an engineer was already on display as early as 1954. Here's his own "kneeler" design, powered by a Rennsport motor.

< Fath & Wohlgemuth flying over the Isle of Man's Ballaugh Bridge, in 1960.

wieder Weltmeister 1956

Zum 3. Mal gelang es BMW in ununterbrochener Folge mit den Weltklasse-Fahrern Noll/Cron den höchsten Titel des internationalen Motorradrennsports zu erringen. BMW Fahrer gewannen überall in neuer Rekordzeit fünf der sechs für die Weltmeisterschaft gewerteten klassischen Rennen:

ENGLISCHE TOURIST TROPHY
GROSSER PREIS VON BELGIEN
GROSSER PREIS VON DEUTSCHLAND
GROSSER PREIS VON HOLLAND
GROSSER PREIS VON ULSTER

sidecar driver as well as a solo rider), had come close to winning the world championship several times before. With two titles now to their name, the pair vowed to go for a third consecutive overall victory. In the very first race of the '67 season, however—and shortly after being cleared of wrongdoing in the TT fuel scandal—they crashed in the Hairpin at Mallory Park, and Scheidegger was killed.

Schneider had retired, and Wohlgemuth, Cecco, Scheidegger, and Camathias—who had been killed in October 1965 in a crash at Brands Hatch—were truly gone. It should be noted that Camathias was killed in a non-championship race, as was the case with many of the crashes described in this chapter. This was the time of the "Continental Circus"; there were only about half a dozen world championship rounds per season, but most racers raced for money almost every weekend.

Racing fans had lost a slew of top riders in chillingly short order, and it was a development that, in cold, technical terms, left the field wide open. Into the vacuum stepped the fledgling team of Klaus Enders and passenger Ralf Engelhardt. Although the partnership was relatively new,

Enders—a former junior champion—was not, and his experience took the pair to a fourth-place finish in their very first Isle of Man TT (in '67) while on their way to the Sidecar World Championship. The Enders kneeler machine now featured Dieter Busch-prepared engines, a rear tire that had widened to car-tire-sized proportions, a short steering column, and a U-link pivoted front fork.

In 1968, Helmut Fath, who'd made a return to sidecar racing a few years earlier, won with a chassis and motor of his own design. The motor was a modern, four-cylinder, dual overhead-cam design that was mounted across the frame. It was branded a URS.

In '69 and '70, the championship again went to Enders (passengered first by Engelhardt and later by Kalauch). At the end of the 1970 season, Enders decided to try his hand at car racing.

The temporary absence of Enders allowed Horst Owesle and Peter Rutterford to win the 1971 world championship on another Fath-designed combo. (The outfit was built by Fath but labeled a Munch, as they were sponsored by the idiosyncratic German motorcycle builder Friedl Munch. It had nothing whatsoever in common

Max Deubel and Emil Horner were almost untouchable in the mid-'60s, despite the fact that Deubel preferred to sit on his motorcycle instead of lying on it. Note the square-profile tire; by this time, sidecar lap times were benefiting from the adoption of tires with automotive profiles and construction.

< "For the third time in an unbroken sequence," reads this '56 poster, "BMW won the highest title in international motorcycle racing with world-class drivers Noll/Cron." BMW in fact took five of the six races ranked for the world championship that year.

with the Munch Mammoth motorcycle, which was powered by an NSU car engine.)

In 1972, Enders ended his brief flirtation with car racing and returned to sidecars. He may have been influenced by car construction, however, as he soon appeared racing a monocoque construction sidecar outfit that finally and completely rejected any of the old "motorcycle frame" influence. Certainly a modern chassis for a tuned Rennsport motor that, despite extensive updating by Bosch engineers, was still a 20-year old-design!

When he finally retired, Klaus Enders had notched twenty-seven Grand Prix wins as a BMW rider, and BMW itself had earned the world championship nineteen times in twenty-one years—a record that still stands. Following the 1974 sidecar season, Enders and BMW retired together. The company had actually ceased fielding a factory team after the reign of Deubel and Horner had come to an end, so its retirement was more poetic than literal. There may have been an accidental benefit to this belt-tightening, however, for when the company stopped supporting the Rennsport motors used by so many privateer sidecar racers, independent shops like Krauser began rebuilding

The chemistry between driver and passenger is difficult to quantify, but it's certainly there. When Scheidegger teamed up with Robinson for the '65 season, it proved to be a recipe for world championships.

< Drivers Fritz Scheidegger (at left, with passenger John Robinson) and Florion Camathias (at right) were often Deubel's toughest rivals.

Enders & Engelhardt push off the start line at the Isle of Man TT in 1967.

motors, thus bringing fresh tuning perspectives to the old boxer twin. Those tuners are still in business today, providing everything from luggage to complete, high-performance transformations of contemporary BMWs.

But with Enders, it turned out, went the last Grand Prix sidecar victory that the marque would claim. Sidecars themselves now held less interest for spectators than they used to, since a plethora of affordable European cars (the Volkswagen in BMW's domestic market, the Citroen 2CV in France, and the Fiat 500 in Italy) were now the working man's basic transport.

During the early '70s, the two-stroke motors that had long dominated the smaller classes came to the fore in the 500cc classes, too. For a while, the Rennsport motor's inherent reliability allowed Enders to win while the two-strokes seized around him, but it was just a question of time before the new (mostly Japanese) motors were durable enough to last a race distance.

The last year in which a four-stroke motor won the 500cc solo championship was 1974, when Phil Read took the title on an MV Agusta. The writing was well and truly on the wall for the four-strokes, and Enders' final championship, too, came that season. It had been a heck of a run for the Rennsport, but in paddocks around the world, the two-strokes had arisen. Falkenhausen, for one, wanted no part of them.

Curiously, few sidecar drivers were able to effectively make the transition to automobile racing. After trying autos, Enders returned to the Sidecar World Championships in 1972.

The passion endures

The rise of the two-strokes in world championship competition meant the end of several eras. Both 500cc classes, sidecars and 500 GP, saw Yamaha and Suzuki become dominant forces. BMW and MV Agusta had owned their respective categories, but they faced the choice of either building two-strokes or giving up their world championship teams. Even mighty Honda, with its limitless racing budget, could not compete with the two-strokes.

In 1969, BMW closed its Munich motorcycle assembly line and opened a new factory on the outskirts of Berlin. The company took advantage of the new facility to launch the /5 series, including the 750cc R 75/5. The new 750 may not have offered quite the performance of the Triumph and BSA triples, and it was definitely overshadowed by the Honda 750-Four, but the R 75 did combine good handling and speed with typical BMW reliability. It quickly found favor in production racing

After a long period during which BMW had heavily invested in the car side of its business, it was finally time for motorcycles to get a new factory in the suburbs of Berlin.

>Ah, the Seventies! Men were men—and had the mustaches and sideburns to prove it—and women were … models. In truth, the R 75/5 was not that sexy, so the company chose instead to race it.

classes, until BMW riders could get their hands on the R 90 S a few years later.

BMWs were especially effective in long, grueling events like the Production TT on the Isle of Man. It was as though the TT organizers were establishing displacement limits in conference with Munich: the Production TT included 750cc machines while the R 75/5 was the fastest production BMW, and they raised the displacement limit to 1000cc just in time for the arrival of the R 90 S!

Helmut Dahne is the BMW rider most closely associated with these epic TTs. Dahne was a track tester for Metzeler, so one imagines he got plenty of seat time. In the first year of the R 90 S (which was introduced as a 1974 model at the Paris show in late '73), the lean and racy-looking Dahne finished third in the Production TT behind the rather more zaftig Hans-Otto Butenuth, also on an R 90 S. It was the best TT result for a BMW two-wheeler since before the war.

In the mid-'70s, Production TT races were run by two-rider teams over ten laps of the Mountain course—more than 375 miles of racing. In those longer races, Dahne and Butenuth paired up. One wonders how they chose suspension settings.

>Ah, nearly seventy! Alexander von Falkenhausen was a motorcycle racer, an F-1 car designer, and head of BMW's racing efforts before ultimately taking charge of all BMW engine development. Here he is on an R 90 S, one of the last BMW models released before he retired at the age of 68.

BMW motorcycles had performed well in endurance racing since long before Dahne's day. In the late '50s, the R 69 S was a stalwart machine, but in the early '60s, the FIM changed endurance-racing rules, moving the focus from production-based machines to sports prototypes. It was not until the advent of the R 90 S that BMW again offered a competitive platform. The ultimate endurance race then (as now) was the Bol d'Or, in France.

Gus Kuhn, a large London motorcycle dealership, had been a major sponsor/builder/entrant of Nortons. When Norton began to collapse, the shop built R 90 S endurance racers—mostly just thoroughly prepared stock bikes.

Krauser was also an entrant. Although the company is best known for its luggage, it also made a four-valve head conversion for boxer twins. In the heyday of its endurance racing team, Krauser also built its own frames, which were spaceframes similar to the ones seen on contemporary Ducatis. These were fitted with highly modified R 90 S and later R 100 RS motors, and raced in FIM World Endurance Championship events.

Krauser's wild specials were outdone by a

handful of machines built by Werner Fallert. Fallert's frame was a more conventional-looking unit, but his motors eschewed almost all factory components. Taking little more than inspiration from an R 100 RS motor, Fallert converted it from a two-valve-per-cylinder OHV design to a four-valve overhead cam unit. Like the old works racers, his cams were bevel-driven. Where Krauser and many others had improved ground clearance by raising the motor, shortening the cylinders, and chamfering the valve covers, Fallert actually changed the cylinder axes, turning the motor into a 170-degree shallow vee. This was surely God's way of telling Fallert that he had too much time on his hands!

>*Helmut Dahne rounds the deceptively tricky downhill right at Governor's Bridge, during the 1976 Production TT.*

Butler & Smith go racing

When people think of BMWs and racing nowadays, what comes to mind—at least in North America—are the told and retold tales of Reg Pridmore and the introduction of the R 90 S. Pridmore rode that production-based bike to the first-ever AMA Superbike Championship in 1976, but that championship didn't come out of the blue. New Jersey-based Butler & Smith (then the U.S. BMW importer) built several F-1 bikes in the early '70s, and the research and development that went into those machines allowed BMW to hit the ground running when the Superbike Championship was set up.

It's interesting to note that in the early '70s, BMW experienced a marketing problem with the introduction of the R 75/5. It was not a full-on sport bike (the Kawasaki Z1 was about to reshape that landscape), but it was also a little too sporty for the pipe-and-tweed-jacket types. It's hard to

believe now that such chrome-sided "toaster" tank bikes are quaint and collectible, but at the time, many of BMW's core customers found the new bike fast and (far too) flashy. Hard-core riders were more inclined to choose an even sportier Japanese four or British triple—the same bikes dominating the Daytona 200 in the early '70s—and that trend gave someone at BMW the idea that racing the new beemer might legitimize it in the eyes of riders who hadn't previously thought of sporting a roundel.

The R 75/5 did well in production racing classes both in Europe and the U.S. Thus encouraged, Munich sent Butler & Smith four racing frames that the firm had developed around its lead rider, Helmut Dahne. "Try racing these," B&S was told, which would not have been much good if the importer didn't have Udo Gietl on staff.

Udo was born in Germany but grew up in the

Designed by Hans-Gunther von der Marwitz, the R 75/5 was a fundamentally well-handling motorcycle, its frame inspired by the famous Manx Norton "Featherbed."

Gietl's first F-1 motorcycle, built up on one of the frames sent from Germany.

United States. At the age of 19—in 1957 or '58—he helped a friend rebuild a BMW R 68. When he walked into Butler & Smith to pick up new main bearings, someone there asked, "Do you know what to do with these?"

"Sure," said Udo.

"When you get finished, bring the bike in," said the B&S man.

When the importer saw that he'd done a competent job, he was hired. Udo worked there until he was drafted, then spent time in Korea repairing communications gear in a remote depot. (Thankfully, the Korean war itself was long over.) After his tour of duty, he studied electronics on the G.I. Bill and then took a job with Hewlett-Packard, working on space projects for a couple of years. He spent a lot of time at Cape Canaveral (yes, he was a rocket scientist) and raced dirt bikes whenever he got the chance. His own racing probably helped him hone the skills that took him from merely being a mechanic to being a real race tuner/builder.

By the late '60s, he was back at Butler & Smith—nominally as a parts manager, but he had the confidence of the business owner, who was also an avid race fan. On the weekends, Udo also spent a lot of time in the machine shop at Amol Precision, a large bike shop in New Jersey that had an active racing program. That was where he met Todd Shuster, a brilliant machinist and fabricator who would assist him for approximately twenty years.

When those four frames arrived from Germany, it was naturally up to Udo to turn them into race bikes. By then, he already knew what he needed to do to liberate some impressive power from boxer twin motors, and it was not long before two of the four frames had been built up, with one going to Kurt Liebmann (the son of Oscar Liebmann, owner of Amol Precision) and the other to Reg Pridmore—an ex-pat Englishman racing out in California.

The problem was, the bikes handled poorly. "It just wouldn't turn," Pridmore recalled years later. "It was like racing a chopper." Gietl didn't even bother building up the other two German frames. Instead, he got Jeff Cole and Steve Jentges (of then-newly formed C&J Racing Frames) to try their hands at a frame design. Their frame was patterned on the original and slightly stiffer—it was

It wasn't until Rob North adapted the frame he'd designed for Triumph and BSA triples that the Butler & Smith project really took off.

made from chromoly instead of mild steel—but didn't work much better.

The third time, however, was the charm. In 1974, Pridmore introduced B&S to another English refugee named Rob North. North had built quite a few frames (and a hell of a good reputation) for Triumph Trident/BSA Rocket III triples. Udo sent Rob a set of cases, and Rob set to work on them.

North recalls, "The basic geometry—the shape and style of the frame—was similar to the ones I was making for the triples. We moved the engine up and forward, and lengthened the swingarm."

That did the trick, and North built two of them. One stayed on the West Coast (North was based in San Diego) for Reg Pridmore, and the other was shipped back to the East Coast, where Gary Fisher raced it. In spite of the inevitable shaft-jacking and the challenges of unsprung weight at the rear, the North/BMW was one of best-handling race bikes in the premiere class (which at the time was not Superbike, but the far more wide-open Formula 750/F-1 class). It might come as a surprise, but the BMW was actually lighter than either of the Yamaha or Suzuki two-strokes it raced against.

>Here, Gary Fisher shows the impressive cornering clearance achieved by North's frame (which raised the engine slightly) and Gietl's shortened cylinders. In the final evolution of the Butler & Smith racers, Gietl would add an anti-dive system to the front end, improving clearance still further.

Butler & Smith had purchased their own dyno in 1970, so by the winter of '74-'75, Udo had really worked the bugs out of the R 75 motor. For increased cornering clearance, the cylinders were dramatically shortened. Short rods terminated in custom pistons with a very high wrist-pin, and the overall width of the motor was reduced by a couple of inches. The motors revved to a reliable 10,500 rpm.

Having moved the redline about 50 percent higher than the stock motor, there were four principal engineering challenges left to solve. Friction losses were addressed with better bearings throughout the motor, while oiling was improved by switching to a smaller oil pump that was less prone to cavitation, and by incorporating a tiny reservoir in the crankshaft journals. (At peak revs, the stock oil pump drew five horsepower!)

In BMW's trademark boxer twin design, the two pistons move in opposite directions. This has obvious primary balance advantages, but the downside is pumping losses. (As the pistons move in and out, crankcase pressures increase and decrease, sapping power.) In the final iteration of his

A few years after the introduction of the R 75/5, BMW introduced the R 90 S. There is, as they say, no replacement for displacement.

race bikes, Udo built a high-volume crankcase breather that fed into a large airbox, with the whole affair controlled by an ingenious reed valve array.

On the intake side, the ports and valves were opened up and straightened as much as the base castings would allow, with input from Jerry Branch (his company, Branch Flowmetrics, is legendary in the world of hot-rods). Todd Shuster, Udo's partner in crime, said, "At the races I'd take the heads off and do a valve job in the motel room. There was almost no aluminum left in them!" To help the motor exhale, headers were gradually tapered to larger diameters.

Taken to its limits, the motor produced nearly 100 horsepower—about all that can come from a two-valve, pushrod twin. (If one considers the XR750 Harleys used in Grand National flat track, it becomes clear they've never made much more than that even after an additional three decades of development.)

The BMW was being raced against Yamaha TZ750s with approximately 40 additional horses, so it still needed every possible advantage in handling and aerodynamics. Since Butler & Smith had

BMW utterly dominated the 1976 Daytona Superbike race. Pridmore, McLaughlin, and Fisher might look like they were running to "team orders" in this picture, but they were racing hard. Fisher dropped out with a leaking oil cooler while McLaughlin won the race in a photo-finish, but it was Pridmore who took the championship.

McLaughlin's bike was set up with a single rear shock, although Pridmore preferred a traditional twin-shock swingarm. The next year, the AMA made it a moot point by clarifying the rules, and all the bikes were converted back to the stock layout.

>In the late '70s, there were some trick BMWs being raced in the AMA, as evidenced by this evocative pit garage scene.

no access to a wind tunnel, Udo bought Honda and Yamaha fairings, then spliced them together to make one that would fit his bike. "I figured they'd done the wind-tunnel testing for me," he said.

In what was probably the most impressive display of the bike's potential, Gary Fisher qualified beside Kenny Roberts (on a TZ750) at the 1975 Laguna Seca national. "And it was reliable!" Udo recalled. Ironically, while Fisher hounded KR Sr. during the race, he had to retire with a blown shock.

Udo had an even more potent F-1 motor on the dyno back at Butler & Smith—one with fuel injection, ram air induction, and a dry sump. It was never raced, however, primarily because Butler & Smith saw the writing on the wall and realized that the F-1 class was destined to become a playground in which the Yamaha TZ750 was a big bully. Luckily, BMW had recently introduced the R 90 S, and when the AMA brought in the production-based Superbike class, much of Udo's F-1 research and development could be applied to an R 90 S Superbike.

Despite the fact that the class had originally been called "Superbike Production," the rules were quite a bit looser back then. The new 900cc BMW models were summarily punched out to 1000cc. They got the same slimming regime, too, with the short rods. In fact, almost all the F-1 development was transferred over.

In theory, the frames of the Butler & Smith R 90 S bikes originated as production items. Gusseting and stiffening the frames with added material was permitted, so Udo and fabricator Todd Shuster added a pair of diagonal frame members that connected the steering head to the swingarm pivot. This allowed them to hang the motor in the frame and cut one of the lower "cradles" so that the motors could be quickly dropped from the frame for servicing.

"The worst thing you could ever do with Udo Gietl," Shuster said with obvious admiration, "was give him a rule book." Udo's rulesmanship was enhanced by his status as a member of the AMA's rules committee. Some of his rivals were surprised to see that while the production R 90 S was a twin shocker, the Butler & Smith Superbike had the same monoshock as the F-1 bike. It turned out that all the manufacturers wanted to be able to move the top mounting points for their rear shocks forward, converting them to "laydown" designs.

< Kurt Liebmann on another very trick boxer, with an overhead cam kit. Note the bevel drive to the head.

The laydown shocks gave them more rear suspension compliance for a given amount of shock travel, reducing heat buildup and foaming. Yamaha had (re)introduced monoshocks to motorcycle racing a few years earlier, but their system still used a long-travel shock up under the gas tank. Udo went to Koni and got a modern, short travel shock that had been developed for an F-1 car, and mounted it under the seat, more like the way it's done today. "If only I'd patented that idea!" he lamented.

The other teams were dumbfounded when Udo's monoshockers cleared tech. According to the rules, however, the position of the rear shocks could be revised. As Shuster put it, "Udo positioned one of the shocks under the seat, and the other one on a shelf in our garage."

The original shock mounts were left intact, and as Pridmore preferred the twin shocks, he raced a more stock-looking bike. For the next season, the rule was clarified, and the bikes thereafter all bore a closer resemblance to their production cousins.

The lessons learned from the F-1 program paid off handsomely in that first Superbike season. Steve McLaughlin won the first race at Daytona,

The R 90 S superbike frame had a diagonal brace connecting the steering head to the swingarm pivot, as inspired by Rob North's F-1 frame.

>McLaughlin lifts the skirt of the R 90 S superbike. Note the twin-plug head.

By 1978, Butler & Smith had "officially" withdrawn from AMA Superbike competition, so Gietl and Schuster created their own G+S team. Gietl devised an anti-dive system that transferred braking torque forces to the steering head.

>John Long continued to race that final version in Battle of the Twins events well into the early '80s.

with Reg Pridmore hot on his trail. Pridmore won the second race, at Laguna Seca; Steve was DNF.

The Achilles' heel of the R 90 S superbike was its crank: It was only supported at the ends—there was no middle bearing to stiffen it—and thus it was bound to flex at high revs. Remember those shortened rods? Udo had reduced the rod length from 135mm to 125mm, which meant there was enough clearance for the piston skirts at bottom dead center, up to a point. Nonetheless, Pridmore won the third and final race, too, at the old Ontario track. That was the only race at which all three BMW Superbikes finished, with McLaughlin and Fisher in third and fourth.

The next year, Butler & Smith stopped racing, although Peter Adams, the company owner, tacitly encouraged Udo to field a few bikes. They had no luck with McLaughlin at Daytona that year, although Ron Pierce won a national at Laconia, essentially a "home race" for B&S. In '78, John Long finished on the Superbike podium at Daytona, after which Udo sold that bike and a spare motor to recoup some of the costs. It showed up in BOTT races until well into the '80s.

Dave Emde, an ex-AMA 250 GP champion, was another BOTT regular. He campaigned a bike sponsored by San Jose BMW, a dealership that is still actively building, racing, and winning on boxer twins.

< In 1981, Emde not only won the BOTT race at Loudon, but was so fast in the wet that San Jose BMW also entered him in the Superbike race. As a late entry, he started at the back of the grid but still ran as high as third. He was finally passed by Freddie Spencer, but he nearly finished on the podium.

Lost and found, in the desert

Right about the time that the lights were going down on BMW's U.S. Superbike presence, the curtain was opening on the next great racing role for the robust boxer twins. In fact, BMW was about to introduce an entirely new category of motorcycle: "adventure" bikes.

Fate works in strange ways. In 1977, a French motorcycle racer named Thierry Sabine entered the Abidjan-Nice rally. The course covered miles of trackless sand dunes in the Sahara desert, and somewhere in Libya, Sabine got off track. He was stranded, lost, and out of fuel; indeed, he was out of hope and almost out of time when he was finally rescued.

Many normal people would have chosen never to return to the desert after such an experience, but not Thierry Sabine. He may simply have been delirious, but according to Sabine, he'd had a near-religious experience out there. He returned to

For years, BMW had performed well in the International Six Day Trial. Although its machines were often a handful in rough terrain, they more than made up in reliability what they gave away in weight.

>Until the 1970s, the ISDT also included road and speed tests that played into BMW's hand. Once the ISDT became the International Six Day Enduro, however, BMW felt that it no longer showcased its motorcycles' all-around strengths.

France filled with a passion for the stark and unforgiving beauty of those empty places, and was determined to find a way to share his desert epiphany. France eagerly listened to his story and was quickly caught up in his dream, perhaps because much of North Africa had once been a patchwork of French colonies.

Sabine imagined an epic race for both cars and motorcycles, going from Paris south across the Sahara desert, then west all the way to the Atlantic Ocean at Dakar, Senegal. He drafted his friend Jean-Claude Morellet to help him. Morellet was better known under the pen name "Fenouil" to many readers of the popular motorcycle magazine *Moto Journal;* he was both a serious journalist and the writer of a wacky comic strip.

Fenouil scouted a route that was approximately 10,000 kilometers long. It began with a short Prologue (so fans in the French capital could see some racing live) near the famous Montlehry circuit in the suburbs of Paris. On the day after Christmas 1978, thousands of Parisians watched the official start from the Place Trocadero, as 80 cars, 90 motorcycles, and a dozen trucks, all competing in a single class, began a transit stage south

through France to Algiers. (Competitors took a ferry across the Mediterranean.) Once on African sand, the race began in earnest, through Algeria, Mali, Niger, Mauritania, and Senegal.

Twenty journalists covered the first running of the Paris-Dakar. Their breathless accounts—including nightly reports broadcast on French television—justified Sabine's slogan, "An adventure for those who participate, a dream for those who stay behind." The nations of France and Belgium were immediately fascinated, and it was not long before the rest of the motorcycling world paused every January to watch and dream about what was, without question, the world's most arduous motor race.

That first Paris-Dakar was won by Cyril Neveu on Yamaha's well-developed XT500. Interestingly, Fenouil, who knew the course and its rigors better than anyone, chose to enter the race on a trick 800cc BMW R 75 prepared by Arcueil Motor and the German BMW expert (and ISDT competitor) Herbert Schek. The only other BMW in the field was entered by another French journalist, Philippe Jambert, who rode a BMW R 65 that was extensively modified with the addition of … a windscreen.

The race saw an attrition rate of almost 60 percent, and neither Fenouil nor Jambert were among the finishers. But the Paris-Dakar was truly the ultimate adventure, and it would not be long before it provided a stage on which BMW could strut its ultimate adventure bike: the BMW GS.

Thierry Sabine's timing was perfect for BMW. The company was already experimenting with "giant trail bikes" by competing in the European enduro championship and at the International Six Day Trial, but it was frustrated by changes at the ISDT. At one time that event had been called "the Olympics of motorcycling" and was seen as the ultimate all-around test of both motorcycle and rider. But when it became the ISDE—with that "E" standing for "enduro"—BMW's engineers and marketing staff all felt that the event had lost its value. The engineers felt it was no longer a practical test of real-world motorcycles, and the marketing department felt the event had lost its cachet as a promotional tool. Based on market research, they knew that dual-sport motorcycles only spent two percent of their time off-road; the other 98 percent was spent on roads of one kind or another, ranging from highways to farm lanes. When

< This early G/S publicity shot emphasizes single-track capability …

… even though the company's market research had established that the vast majority of dual-sport riding was actual done on asphalt.

the ISDE became a pure enduro that could only be won on a single minded "dirt bike," BMW bowed out. Luckily, they saw the Paris-Dakar as the perfect showcase for their fast, powerful, tough boxer twins.

Fenouil was back on a BMW for the 1980 edition of the race. This time, there was an official BMW team sponsored by all of the French BMW dealers, and Hubert Auriol was also riding for them. The bikes were prepared by HPN (a German specialist tuner that is still in the business of building fast boxers for rough country).

Once again, the bikes displaced just under 800cc. With a 9.3:1 compression ratio, they were good for about 55 hp at 7,000 rpm. Above the motor sat a cavernous 38-liter fuel tank, and at the rear, the swingarm was still double-sided but suspension was provided via a single Bilstein shock. The long-travel front forks came from a big Maico enduro bike, while the wheels and tires (21-inch front, 18-inch rear) were the same units Akront and Dunlop sold for motocross use. Although Auriol was sidelined with a gearbox failure late in the race, Fenouil finished an impressive fifth overall, behind four Yamahas.

The first version of the Gelände/Strasse was a two-wheeled SUV inspired by the Paris-Dakar.

>In this photo, a lightweight monolever rear end is being race-prepped in the HPN workshop.

That fall, BMW took advantage of the press attention it had received for racing in the desert to introduce the R 80 G/S. The initials stood for *Gelände Strasse*, meaning "offroad and street" in German. Although the first R 80 was noteworthy for its "monolever" single-sided swingarm with integral driveshaft, the bike, in most other ways, bore a strong family resemblance to Fenouil's and Auriol's racers.

The G/S (later simply GS) was originally introduced as a niche product. The company expected to sell a few to genuine adventurers, but it became a signature BMW model when far less adventurous motorcyclists realized that the same traits that made the bike suitable for transcontinental off-road rallies also made it supremely competent and confidence-inspiring in day-to-day riding. As Thierry Sabine had realized, "Those who stay behind, dream," and the dreams were all the more vivid from the saddle of a G/S. "Today I'm just commuting to work," the typical G/S rider told himself, "but if the boss crosses me, tomorrow I'll ride to Tierra del Fuego."

A few months after the official launch of the R 80 G/S, the third edition of the Paris-Dakar

The message in this publicity photo seems to be that the full Paris-Dakar kit will get you well beyond the reach of any mother-in-law.

added a few countries to the route, passing through France, Algeria, Mali, Upper Volta, and the Ivory Coast before turning back north into Senegal. The official BMW team was made up of Auriol, Fenouil, and a French motorcycle cop named Bernard Neimer. Their bikes were again prepared by HPN; the most obvious visual difference from a stock G/S was the double-sided swingarm, with a single laterally mounted Bilstein shock giving an impressive 9-plus inches of rear-wheel travel. There were an additional six privateers on BMWs, too, whereas before almost all the privateers had chosen Yamaha XT500s. The roundel was about to shove the tuning forks aside!

Even by Dakar standards, that third race was brutal. Two thirds of the cars were abandoned, and attrition was even worse among the bikes: 106 started, 28 finished. In an environment where even a finish was a victory, BMW experienced true triumph: Auriol won the race, Fenouil finished a creditable fourth, and Neimer came in seventh. (Honda and KTM, future race winners, also appeared in the top ten.)

One would assume that after HPN-prepped machines recorded a 100-percent finishing record in that tough '81 race, the German shop would be called upon to build BMW's 1982 contenders, too. The contract instead went to Arcueil Motor, in France, and the bikes were plagued with gearbox problems. (In fairness to the French shop, however, that probably had more to do with the extra power generated by motors that had been punched out to 980cc.)

By about the midpoint of the '82 edition, Hubert Auriol was forced to retire, and with no spare gearbox parts left, the BMW team convinced the remaining runners that it would be unsafe to press on. A year after the high of 1981, there was not a single stage win or finisher on a G/S.

The next year, Arcueil again prepped the official bikes, and again, the factory bikes used a double-sided swingarm. This time, instead of a single Bilstein shock, the bikes featured a more conventional (at the time) layout with twin Ohlins.

The 1982 motors were built by Herbert Schek, a German who knew the boxers as well as anyone, and rode them well, too. With Schek's fettling, the 980cc twins produced more than 70 horsepower. (That was plenty, given the tires and suspensions of the day.) That power came from burning plenty

Besides earning racing laurels, the G/S (later, GS) series of motorcycles also became de rigeur for the most extreme globetrotters. Author and photojournalist Helge Pedersen spent ten years circumnavigating the globe on his R 80 G/S, then traded it to the BMW collection for a newer model.

of fuel; Arcueil had managed to shoehorn an extra couple of gallons of gas into an underseat tank.

BMW desperately needed some luck after its "no finish" 1982 result. Imagine, then, how the team felt when its lead rider, Hubert Auriol, crashed and broke his arm while on a reconnaissance ride in mid-December. Nonetheless, Auriol not only started the race eighteen days later; he *won* it eighteen days and 12,000 km after that.

The following season proved to be perhaps *the* defining year for the big BMW adventure bikes in this epic race. Now fitted with engines of over 1000cc, the boxers made more than 75 hp, necessitating an auxiliary oil cooler in the desert heat. HPN got the contract to prepare the factory bikes, and Gaston Rahier, a Belgian, joined Frenchmen Auriol and Loizeaux on the official squad. It was Rahier who won the race, with he and Auriol winning twelve of the eighteen stages between them. Auriol finished second and Loizeaux, fifth. It was a completely dominant performance.

It was no wonder that, later that year, BMW released a special R 80 G/S Paris-Dakar model. Compared to a stock G/S, the "Dakar" had a larger fuel tank (with Gaston Rahier's signature on

In the late '80s, the famous "bumblebee" paint scheme seemed to warn strangers that this was a serious motorcycle.

< Gaston Rahier poses with his race bike and a Paris-Dakar replica.

RALLY PARIJS-DAKAR 1988.
DE WINNAAR VAN DE MARATHONKLASSE OP BMW.

e berijder:
ddy Hau op BMW.

e kleding:
MW Endurokleding
akar.

e motorfiets:
PN BMW R 80 G/S
edstrijduitvoering.

This poster (in Flemish) was one of many advertising efforts that leveraged BMW's impressive—and to many motorcyclists, surprising—success in grueling off-road races.

>*In some ways, the schedule of a "Dakar" is almost as punishing as the racing; among other hardships, riders suffer weeks of severe sleep deprivation. Here, BMW single-cylinder racer Oscar Gallardo prepares to set off long before dawn. Gallardo was originally going to ride a twin, but when he failed to get along with that bike, Jimmy Lewis was drafted to ride it.*

it) and few other practical touches, like a tough stainless steel exhaust system and a larger battery that was exposed for easy access. Most of the other changes were cosmetic, but while it resembled the factory bikes, it was more than 120 pounds heavier than the one Rahier actually rode. (That's only appropriate; the factory team was sponsored by *Penthouse* magazine, so the bikes were obviously stripped!)

Rahier won again the next year. Hubert Auriol had been lured away from the roundel to Cagiva, and although he managed to win a stage on his Italian machine, he did not finish the race.

Then, in 1986, disaster struck the Paris-Dakar: Event founder Thierry Sabine was killed in a helicopter crash in the desert. Although the event had grown into a massive logistical and media exercise involving hundreds of people—and was broadcast to millions in real time—the "Dakar" had sprung from Thierry Sabine's imagination and had remained his personal creation. When he died, the event lost its innocence. The organizing committee rallied, and—knowing that Sabine would have wanted the show to go on—they finished the

race. It was a tough year for BMW, too, however; the top finisher was Eddy Hau, in eighth.

In 1987, Rahier finished third overall. Nothing to be ashamed of, but another failure by comparison. Although there continued to be a scattering of privateers on BMW GS models, the factory would not return (even unofficially) for almost a decade.

Remember the guy who started the first Paris-Dakar race on a stock R 65? In 1996, another Frenchman named David Castera started the race (it was the Granada-Dakar that year) on a nearly stock F 650 Funduro. That model, which at the time had a motor sourced from Rotax and was assembled by Aprilia, was only a year or two old. Castera was not part of any official BMW team, but when he finished eleventh overall and first in the "experimental" class, the company was quick to run a few win ads. Why an essentially stock bike could be called experimental is a good question…. Perhaps the experiment was to see if *any* production motorcycle could possibly survive such a grueling test.

There was, however, another competitor in the '96 race who would later be important to BMW.

American journalist Jimmy Lewis finished a very impressive fourth overall in his first attempt at the epic race, albeit on a KTM.

In 1998, BMW returned to the race with a full factory team managed by Richard Schalber, another veteran of BMW's final year of ISDT competition way back in 1979. That was a learning year; the Frenchman Brucy finished well down the order and three of the four F 650s failed to finish at all.

Schalber's team returned the next year with motorcycles that were built from the ground up for the task. Those "Funduros" (officially designated F 650 RRs) displaced 700cc and made 70 hp; they rolled on WP forks and shock, providing almost a foot of travel at each end. According to the French magazine *Moto Verte*, the only stock parts were the taillight and its surrounding plastic cowl.

Richard Sainct emerged the winner, a scant five minutes ahead of the second-place KTM after 9,393 kilometers of racing over seventeen days. This time, all four of the singles finished, too.

In 2000, BMW again fielded Sainct and three other riders on Schalber's singles. The company also contracted with HPN to build a pair of boxer

Andrea Mayer has proven herself to be one of the fastest (and toughest) women in rally-raid racing.

< Jimmy Lewis gets some fast air during the 2000 Paris-Dakar-Cairo rally. The next year, he was caught out in some similar "mega-whoops," badly injuring his wrists—and his chances to become the first American to score a Dakar win.

twins for an Englishman, John Deacon, and Jimmy Lewis. Lewis came as close as any American ever has to winning the event.

Alfred Halbfeld and Klaus Pepperl (respectively the "H" and "P" in HPN) had long been BMW's defacto race shop when it came to building boxer twins for off-road competition. They knew that their motorcycle had to retain the fundamental look of the then-new R 1150 GS, so they focused their efforts on cutting weight and optimizing the big bike's balance (despite the fact that the bikes carried an amazing 54 liters of fuel in no fewer than four fuel tanks). Additionally, they abandoned the telelever front end concept but retained the paralever rear end (although their own take on the basic design resulted in a dramatically reduced unsprung weight).

Although the Dakar was the ultimate prize, Deacon and Lewis rode the machines in a few other rally-raid races as well. To comply with the rules of the Dubai rally, the bikes had to displace under 900cc, which explains why their official designation came to be R 900 GS-RR.

The task of building the special "undersized" motors was outsourced to Helmut Mader. He built

Richard Sainct won the 2000 edition of the rally on an F 650 RR prepared in the factory race shop by Richard Schalber. The actual displacement of the motor was 700cc.

< Here, Mayer is seen at speed on her F 650 RR in the 2000 edition of the race, which was even longer than most, since the route was Paris-Dakar-Cairo.

a limited run of 90 hp motors that gave the boxers a wave of torque that minimized their weight penalty, and also gave them a significant top speed advantage where terrain permitted.

Dubai was a bit of a trial. "Something broke every single day," said Lewis. When it was over, he was skeptical of the machine's ability to survive a Dakar race, but when Lewis reported to Europe for the start of the 2000 event, he was shocked to see that HPN and BMW had addressed every single weakness that had appeared in the early season test.

Despite the surprising agility of the twins, Sainct again won the overall race on a single-cylinder machine. Although Lewis was occasionally able to exploit his top speed advantage (he won three stages), in the end, the twins' 15 hp advantage was not enough to compensate for their 20kg weight disadvantage.

One interesting side-note to Lewis' 2000 race is that late in the race, he lost a lot of time to a broken Paralever torque arm (the alloy strut that runs essentially parallel to the main swingarm) after the part struck a huge rock in the track. "I spent 45 minutes rigging a repair out in the

The R 900 RR was originally built to 900cc capacity to conform to the rules of the Dubai Rally—ninety horsepower was plenty! The cycle parts were prepped by HPN, and the motors by Mader.

< Rally Paris-Dakar-Cairo 2000 - BMW Motorcycle Team Gauloises - standing, from left: Lewis, Sainct, Brucy, Gallardo; overhead is Mayer. They are celebrating Sainct's victory, and their survival.

Rally Paris Dakar 2001 – BMW Motorrad Team
Gauloises. Although he credits his success to his
navigation skills and not his riding, Jimmy Lewis
has also shown a knack for treating the big boxer
like a much smaller "dirt bike."

>This view of the Paralever on a contemporary
HP2 shows the torque arm that was relocated
out of harm's way—a direct example of competition
improving production motorcycles.

desert," said Lewis, "and when I got in, the Germans said, 'This will never happen again.' If you need proof that racing improves production bikes, you'll see that when they redesigned the GS, they moved that strut from below the swingarm to above it." Remarkably, BMW had done a major re-engineering of the component as a result of a single racing incident!

Once again, this time to celebrate the single-cylinder bike's victory, BMW released a "Dakar" special edition. At the same time, BMW repatriated the F 650's manufacture from Italy to Germany, and re-engineered the bike (notably, with fuel injection).

Lewis returned in 2001, even more determined to become the first American to win the world's toughest race. His own toughness was certainly not in question that year: After a bad fall early in the event, he raced several thousand kilometers on two severely sprained wrists; on the final day of the Paris-Dakar, he crashed again and broke his collarbone, but still finished the race. He in fact crossed the finish line in seventh place—surely some kind of moral victory—and was immediately airlifted to the medical center.

So, victory in the Paris-Dakar still eludes America. Recently, arch-rivals KTM have dominated the Paris-Dakar results, but it is BMW that has totally dominated the adventure bike market. It's a niche that would have remained small if it weren't for the very large stage of—and global attention paid to—the world's longest, toughest race.

>Despite the Herculean efforts of Jimmy Lewis, America still awaits its first victory in the world's toughest motorcycle race.

Special series and spec racing

The rise of the K-series inline triples and fours in the mid-'80s, then of the four-valve-per-cylinder "oilhead" boxers in the mid-'90s, took the BMW model line two big steps forward in terms of modernization. Both series, again, were used in endurance racing although they perhaps didn't capture the imaginations of specialty builders and tuners quite as much as the R 90 S had. This may have been because many specials builders are as interested in the extent to which the "donor" machine can be improved as they are in outright victory.

One new BMW that did interest racers was the 650cc single introduced in late 1993. Initially sold as the "Funduro," the name may not have suggested racing applications, but the four-valve, Rotax-built single was immediately of interest to racers in the fast-growing Supermono class. The Supermonos were a support class at European rounds of the World Superbike Championship, so they played to large crowds and attracted quality fields.

Most of the so-called "BMW" Supermono racers, however, were BMWs in name only, as they were Rotax motors installed in frames made by Bimota, Tigcraft, Harris, etc. The ultimate example of this type was the Chrysalis-BMW built and ridden by David Morris. Morris' bikes were built on Tigcraft (later Harris) frames, and he tuned the motors himself, going so far as to carve a new cylinder head from billet. He raced to three victories in the Isle of Man TT's short-lived "Singles" class between 1997-'99.

During this period, the phrase "BMW racing" brought very specific images to mind among racing fans, as the company sponsored a number of spec-racing series in which all competitors raced identically prepared BMW models. During the mid-'90s, for example, the American Historic Racing

Three legends from the Woodstock era, flying in formation at a Daytona Battle of the Legends: In the front row, from left to right, are Yvon Duhamel, Dave Aldana, and Jay Springsteen.

Motorcycle Association (AHRMA) and BMW promoted the Battle of the Legends. These were races between retired racing stars, all mounted on identical boxer twins (R 100 R models in the first year, and then R1100RS bikes). At the sharp end of the field, "Legends" races were real races! The series was shut down when Roger Reimann, an ex-Daytona 200 winner, died during an event. It was believed that he actually died of heart failure, not crash-related injuries, but the company ceased support of racing in North America for several years.

From 1999 to 2004, BMW organized a series called the Boxer Cup, for R1100S machines. This was a bit of a "motorcycle Olympics," with an emphasis on national teams. The U.S. team was comprised of Udo Gietl as tuner and Brian Parriott as rider, and since Boxer Cup races supported European rounds of the MotoGP series, they raced in front of some very large crowds. The Boxer Cup also came to the U.S. in '03 and '04 as part of Daytona's Bike Week, and this series attracted a number of truly talented riders. Although the machines were nominally identical and stock, there

>*While the "Legends" races were largely high-speed parades, the Boxer Cup was hard-core racing!*

was a lot of care and skill lavished on their preparation.

A popular Boxer Cup Replica model was also produced and sold in dealerships. This bike was very well reviewed in many motorcycle magazines as an example of a motorcycle for which the whole exceeded the sum of its parts. Beginning in 2005, the emphasis shifted to the new K 1200 R muscle bike, so BMW promoted the Power Cup, a similar series for that model. It too ran in support of MotoGP races in Europe.

When it came time to hire a rider, Gietl called friends at the powerhouse American Honda superbike team and asked, "If you were given the budget to hire one more rider, who would you hire?" They answered, "Brian Parriott." Here, Parriott is en route to winning at Daytona.

< More power! With the advent of the potent K 1200 R, BMW's spec series was aptly renamed the Power Cup.

Onward and upward

The introduction of the HP2 version of the R 1200 GS reawakened BMW's competitive urges, but the question was, where could such a machine be raced? The company had learned back in the early 1970s that most conventional enduros were too tight and technical for anything wider or heavier than a single-cylinder machine. In Europe, there was the Erzberg Rally; the "main event" there is a hare scramble in which typically less than 10 percent of the competitors reach the finish, but there is also a 14-kilometer hillclimb well suited to the new boxer. In 2007, the twin-cylinder "King's Class" and outright victory went to Simo Kirssi.

Erzberg is held in the Austrian Alps, but there is an even more famous hillclimb in the American Rockies: Pikes Peak. The Pikes Peak course is longer than the Erzberg Prologue, and as it combines asphalt and gravel, it is in many ways the perfect test of an adventure bike.

>The fast, open road of the Prologue of the Erzberg Rodeo is well suited to the big HP2. In 2005, BMW lured its American star of the Paris-Dakar, Jimmy Lewis, to Austria to give it a try.

First Side Car On Pikes Peak Alt. 14147 Ft.
No. 1A Sep 12 1915. Manitou to Summit 2 hr. 15 min.

Although Pikes Peak has often been associated with automobile racing, it has long attracted motorcyclists. Contemporary times are quite a bit faster than the two hours cited on this historic photo. The current course record is well under twelve minutes, although in fairness, the two-hour climb was from a starting point much lower on the mountain.

Pikes Peak is one of the world's oldest and most historic races. (Indeed, the Arapaho Indians who had lived in the mountain's shadow for millennia must have been dumbfounded when U.S. Army Lieutenant Zebulon Montgomery Pike "discovered" Pikes Peak in 1806. After attempting to climb the mountain and being forced back by cold and snow, Pike wrote in his log, "… I believed no human being could have ascended to its pinical [sic].") About 100 years later, a Colorado mining baron named Spencer Penrose built a road up there. In 1916, he offered a trophy for the fastest car or motorcycle ascent, and the Pikes Peak International Hillclimb—also known as the "Race to the Clouds"—was born.

As the course has improved (read: "gotten faster," not "gotten safer") it has become a supermotard rider's version of the Isle of Man TT. The lower part of the course is lined with rocks and trees, and thus the old racer's maxim, "It's not the fall that hurts you, it's the sudden stop," definitely applies. As for the upper part of the course … suffice to say that some of the sheer cliffs give the term "runoff" a whole new meaning.

Like the TT course, Pikes Peak is very hard to

learn, but if anything, "PP" riders get even less opportunity to practice on closed roads. There are only two or three official practice mornings, and because the course is split—with cars using one part of the course while bikes practice on the other—racers don't see the entire course until they actually race on it.

Until 2006, the Pikes Peak class structure for motorcycles topped out at 750cc, but the organizers will allow almost anything to run in the exhibition class. In 2006, exhibition runs were made by a V10 diesel Volkswagen Touareg driven by ex-Indy 500 winner Danny Sullivan; a 300 horsepower quad built on a snowmobile chassis and powered by a turbocharged Yamaha R1 motor; and there was even a demonstration run by a 1000 hp Grand Vitara driven by the President of Suzuki's global motorsports division, Nobuhiro Tajima. There was also a full-factory effort among the exhibition motorcycles; BMW brought a pair of 1200cc HP2 enduro bikes and a Dakar Rally-attitude to the mountain.

The BMWs were ridden by Simo Kirssi and Casey Yarrow. Kirssi (the Finn with the good finishes at Erzberg) is a skilled rider but was out of his

American supermoto rider Casey Yarrow was the fastest of the HP2 riders in 2006.

element on the partially paved course. He spent most of practice looking like he'd rather have been almost anywhere else. The mix of pavement and dirt was familiar ground for Yarrow, however, who's one of the top supermoto riders on the U.S. West Coast.

The bikes made enough power to shred the road racing rain tires that seemed to be the best all-round choice. (Other racers attested to the fact that the BMWs threw more-painful roost than any other bikes on the mountain.) There was, however, no getting around their sheer bulk. During a break in the pits, another supermoto regular asked Yarrow what the HP2 was like to ride. With a shake of his head and shrug he replied, "That's one heavy son of a b—— to get slowed down and turned."

By race day, it was clear that no one was going to set the course record on a motorcycle weighing more than 400 pounds. That said, BMW did have the fastest bikes in the exhibition class. (The class also included two locally made bikes powered by 100-horsepower "Hyland" V-twin motors from Sweden. One of those was ridden by ex-AMA motocross champ Chuck Sun.)

Yarrow's time there would have been the outright motorcycle course record just a few years earlier. BMW's director of motorcycle sport, Berthold Hauser, said, "It gives a good feeling in the heart to be here. I think we must come back."

In 2007, BMW did return to Pikes Peak. In the intervening year, there had been three notable developments: First, the organizers had created an official category—not just an exhibition class—for 1200cc motorcycles; second, a series of hairpin turns high on the mountain, known as "The Ws," had been paved; and third, BMW had developed the Megamoto version of the HP2, with twin front discs and 17-inch wheels. All of those developments served to raise hopes of an outright motorcycle course record.

BMW's '07 assault on the mountain included no fewer than five bikes. Casey Yarrow came back, Kirssi was replaced as the token European by endurance ace Markus Barth, and the three fastest riders on the mountain—AMA Supermoto stars Micky Dymond and the Trachey brothers, Gary and Greg—were hired away from KTM and Husqvarna.

With the added pavement, most riders chose

The Megamoto, with its twin front brake discs and 17-inch wheels, seemed a natural for the Pikes Peak course. The bikes that were raced were almost completely stock—far closer to production items than anything else that raced there.

< "Don't look down" is the advice Pikes Peak veterans give newcomers. It's definitely not a race for riders prone to vertigo.

to use cut slick tires of the type used in supermoto competition. The Megamotos were certainly fast on the pavement, but they overpowered their tires on the unpaved portions. It rained in the days leading up to the race and the unpaved sections were, if anything, looser in the race than they had been in practice. In the end, Gary Trachey came within a few seconds of his old course record, which was highly impressive considering that the motorcycles were stock Megamotos with little more than the headlights, taillights, and turn signals removed! One suspects it will not be long before the outright course record falls to one of these new boxers, and that the newly developed 450cc single will also prove effective on the mountain.

What else does the future hold? The much lighter and more powerful 1200cc boxer motor (which first appeared in GS guise in 2004) has not just opened up racing opportunities for the big adventure bikes; the R 1200 S has—perhaps predictably—again attracted the attention of endurance racers.

In 2007 the factory entered a stripped-and-lightened R 1200 S in the famous 24-hour race at

Open-class motocross legend Joel Smets is also an ISDT gold medalist. Here, he puts a development version of the new 450cc single through its paces during a round of the German enduro championship. As this book goes to press, BMW North America plans an assault on the AMA's cross-country championships, spearheaded by Scott Summers (5-time GNCC champion, 4-time Hare Scrambles champ).

< Gary Trachey scrabbles for grip on one of the unpaved sections. He was already the Pikes Peak course record holder, but he beat his own best time on the Megamoto. Although he was denied the course record when Rotax-mounted Davey Durelle went faster still, there's always next year!

Le Mans. The team was comprised of riders Thomas Hinterreiter, Rico Penzkofer, and Marcus Barth. The race was a round of the official QMMF Endurance World Championship (in which the two principal classes are Superbike and Superstock, for 1000cc machines), so the BMW team had to enter in the sparsely populated "Open" class. In the end, their class win was probably less impressive than their sixteenth overall result, which spoke volumes in a field deep with full-on superbikes and against teams that are vastly experienced in this unique branch of motorcycle racing.

In the fall of 2006, the R 1200 S won the inaugural SunTrust Moto-ST endurance championship round, taking victory over a 34-team field at Daytona International Speedway. Designed specifically for twin-cylinder machines, the Moto-ST series operates within the successful Grand Am structure, and it has offered BMW a perfect platform to return to North American racetracks.

"The decision to participate in Moto-ST was almost instantaneous," said BMW North American Community and Communications Manager Laurence Kuykendall at the time. "Our models are becoming more radical, more powerful, and

With the HP2 Sport, BMW has again produced a real boxer "superbike." Like the legendary R 90 S, it immediately established its racing credentials. Shown here is the official BMW Motorrad Motorsport entry in the 24 Hours of Le Mans.

>"Slow and steady wins the race," they say, but in endurance racing it's more like "Fast and steady wins the race"—even in the pits. This prototype HP2 Sport benefits from its shaft drive (no need for chain adjustments) and single-sided swingarm, which allows for quick wheel changes.

Brian Parriott honed his boxer-riding technique in the Boxer Cup, then put it to good use in the SunTrust Moto-ST endurance series.

lighter, and the feeling is that with our R 1200 S, we again have a BMW with serious performance potential."

Two major teams represented BMW in the debut of the premier, SuperSport Twins class: BMW Cycles Daytona, and San Jose BMW—already a successful force in AFM and the BMW Boxer Cup Series. BMW Cycles Daytona featured two-time world endurance champion Warwick Nolan (an Australian), alongside AMA racers John Haner and Mike Ciccotto. The San Jose squad teamed headliner Stephane Mertens—a Belgian rider with three World Endurance titles to his name—with regular San Jose-rider Brian Parriott and American Nate Kern, another proven rider and past CCS champion. The team was managed by Udo Gietl himself.

At the debut Moto-ST event—which had developed quickly, allowing manufacturers little time to prepare or develop special parts—the BMW race machines were essentially stock bikes; modifications comprised nothing more than a quick-change rear wheel and a change of exhaust. To achieve proper gearing for Daytona, the teams simply used the final drive from a R 1200 RT touring bike, and the results couldn't have been better. Not only did San Jose BMW take the win in commanding fashion, but the two BMW teams were actually each others' own stiffest competition until the #83 of BMW Cycles Daytona ran out of gas on the far side of the racetrack following a rider-crew miscommunication, relegating them to a fourth-place finish. Kuykendall later called the Daytona event "a historic moment for the BMW brand."

After that historic first victory, the San Jose BMW team was a threat to win the first full-season MotoST championship. They had bad luck on their return to Daytona, where they were only able to finish twelfth. But they won at Virginia International Raceway, and stayed at the front until the series reached Iowa Speedway. There, the team decided track conditions were too dangerous. (The wisdom of that decision was emphasized, unfortunately, by two serious injuries on the tight, walled-in layout.)

Giving up any points from the Iowa round effectively took the team out of contention for the championship. But they nearly ended the season (again, at Daytona) on a real high note. The team

October in Daytona is not only for endurance racers. Brad Hendry, sponsored by Foothills BMW, won three races in the season-ending CCS/ASRA "Race of Champions." Hendry and his R 1200 S dominated the GT Lights, Lightweight GP, and Lightweight Superbike classes.

of Parriott, Kern, and Richard Cooper, of England, ran right at the sharp end of the field until 45 minutes from the checkered flag. And again, bad luck struck; Cooper collided with another motorcycle that had run off the track and was re-entering. So, the first MotoST premier-class championship went to Aprilia, just as this book was going to press. "We had what it took to win," said Parriott, "But under the circumstances we were lucky to finish." The legion of boxer fans certainly hasn't heard the last of San Jose BMW!

As welcome as the Moto-ST platform has been for twin-cylinders, it seems the opportunities may not stop there. BMW has long been rumored to be working on an experimental 800cc MotoGP bike, and in June 2007, the organizers of the World Superbike Championship announced that beginning in 2008, twin-cylinder motorcycles of up to 1200cc would be allowed to compete.

Although the AMA Superbike Series will not follow suit in time for the '08 season, it's likely that their rules, too, will eventually be brought into line. Add it all up, and it seems the racing world has cycled back into a time that's ripe for a true BMW return. Perhaps there is, after all, an heir to Reg Pridmore in the wings, destined to join the very long list of BMW racers who've already ridden their way into the history books.

If that proves to be the case, that next champion will owe his success to an even longer line of brilliant thinkers; those who watched their riders' road races, trials events, and record-setting attempts with calculating eyes that looked past the immediate glory, toward what could be done better. Throughout its long life, BMW has been defined by engineers who were not afraid to be unconventional, and who took the lessons of disappointments *and* the inspiration of race wins back to their workshops. Though the results sometimes had to wait for the rest of the world to catch up—often literally, on the racetrack—slowing down has simply never been an option.

Nate Kern, Brian Parriott, and Stephane Mertens
celebrate the first overall win in the inaugural
SunTrust MotoST Endurance Championship. Since
the series is limited to twin-cylinder machines,
the R 1200 S competes for outright victories.

Major race and championship wins

1924
German National Championship (500cc)   Fritz Bieber

1925
German National Championship (250cc)   Josef Stelzer
German National Championship (500cc)   Rudolf Reich

1926
German National Championship (500cc)   Ernst Henne

1927
German National Championship (500cc)   Hans Soenius
German National Championship (750cc)   Ernst Henne
Targa Florio (500cc)   Paul Kppen

1928
German National Championship (500cc)   Hans Soenius
German National Championship (1000cc)   Anton Bauhofer
Targa Florio (500cc)   Ernst Henne

1929
German National Championship (500cc)   Hans Soenius
German National Championship (1000cc)   Josef Stelzer
Targa Florio (500cc)   Paul Kppen

1930
German National Championship (1000cc)   Fritz Wiese

1931
German National Championship (1000cc)   Ralph Roese

1932
German National Championship (1000cc)   Ralph Roese

1933, 1934 and 1935
Winner of the National team award at the ISDT

1935 and 1938
Winner of the Silver-Vase at the ISDT

1937
German National Championship (500cc)   Karl Gall

1938
German National Championship (500cc)   Georg Meier
European Championship (500cc)   Georg Meier

1939
German National Championship (500cc)   Ludwig Kraus
Isle of Man TT (Senior)   Georg Meier

1947
German National Championship (500cc)   Georg Meier

Note: Between 1947 and 1974 BMW also won numerous
championships in 500cc, 600cc, 750cc, and 900cc Classes.

1948
German National Championship (500cc)   Georg Meier

1949
German National Championship (500cc)   Georg Meier

Note: This was the inaugural year of the current FIM
road racing world championship–now known as MotoGP

1950
German National Championship (500cc)   Georg Meier

1951

German National Championship (500cc)   Walter Zeller

1953

German National Championship (500cc)   Georg Meier

1954

German National Championship (500cc)   Walter Zeller
Sidecar World Championship   Noll/Cron

1955

German National Championship (500cc)   Walter Zeller
Sidecar World Championship   Faust/Remmart

1956

German National Championship (500cc)   Ernst Riedelbauch
Sidecar World Championship   Noll/Cron

Note: Walter Zeller posts highest-ever overall ranking for a BMW solo rider in the world championship–second, behind the great John Surtees (MV Agusta)

1957

German National Championship (500cc)   Ernst Hiller
Sidecar World Championship   Hillebrand/Grunwald

1958

German National Championship (500cc)   Ernst Hiller
Sidecar World Championship   Schneider/Straus

Note: In 1958, Ernst Hiller and Dickie Dale both won non-championship Grand Prix races on 500cc BMWs. Those were the last two, of at least 35, victories in Classic races dating back to 1925.

1959

German National Championship (500cc)   Ernst Hiller
Sidecar World Championship   Schneider/Straus

1960

Sidecar World Championship   Fath/Wohlgemuth

1961

German National Championship (500cc)   Hans Guenther Jaeger

The changing of the guard: Hockenheim, 1954. Schneider & Strauss (#34) are on their production BMW RS54 sidecar combination, Noll & Cron (#43) are seen with their BMW works combination along-side Oliver & Nutt (#42) on a Norton. Oliver was an innovator who was always seeking ways of overcoming his Norton's lack of top-end power. He was the first driver to race a "kneeler" and one of the first to exploit streamlining.

< Hillebrand & Grunwald finished second to Oliver & Nutt (Norton) in their first TT appearance in '54, but they won on the Isle of Man the next two years.

Sidecar World Championship	Deubel/Hörner

1962

German National Championship (500cc)	Ernst Hiller
Sidecar World Championship	Deubel/Hörner

1963

Sidecar World Championship	Deubel/Hörner

1964

Sidecar World Championship	Deubel/Hörner

1965

Sidecar World Championship	Scheidegger/Robinson

1966

Sidecar World Championship	Scheidegger/Robinson

1967

Sidecar World Championship	Enders/Englehardt

1969

Sidecar World Championship	Enders/Englehardt

1970

Sidecar World Championship	Enders/Englehardt

1972

Sidecar World Championship	Enders/Englehardt

1973

Sidecar World Championship	Enders/Englehardt

1974

Sidecar World Championship	Enders/Englehardt

1976

AMA Superbike National (Daytona)	Steve McLaughlin
AMA Superbike National (Monterey)	Reg Pridmore
AMA Superbike National (Riverside)	Reg Pridmore
AMA Superbike Championship	Reg Pridmore
Isle of Man (Production TT 1000cc)	Helmut Dhne

Noll & Cron (shown here at the 1954 Sidecar World Championship awards ceremony) may not look like testosterone-charged motorcycle racers, but they were the faces of the next period of BMW domination.

>Enders & Engelhardt's '67 world championship marked the fourteenth consecutive world championship win for the Bavarian manufacturer.

1977
AMA Superbike National (Loudon)   Ron Pierce

1978
AMA Superbike National (Loudon)   Harry Klinzmann

1981
Dakar Rally   Hubert Auriol

1983
Dakar Rally   Hubert Auriol

1984
Dakar Rally   Gaston Rahier

1985
Dakar Rally   Gaston Rahier

1986
AMA Battle of the Twins (Loudon, NH)   Bert Stuckert

*Note: Stuckert finished second overall in
'86 AMA Battle of the Twins championship.*

1997
Isle of Man TT (Singles)   Dave Morris

1998
Isle of Man TT (Singles)   Dave Morris

1999
Dakar Rally   Richard Sainct
Isle of Man TT (Singles)   Dave Morris

2000
Dakar Rally   Richard Sainct

index

Laurel C. Allen

Laurel Allen grew up in the road race paddocks of North America, the daughter of a two-time Canadian national champion and twenty-five-year fixture on the AMA road race scene. Raised in the shadow of road race legends and alongside many of the fastest competitors racing today, it's no surprise Allen eventually sought her own place in the industry, starting out a lowly summer peon at *Cycle News* and ending up—thirteen years later—Senior Editor of *Road Racer X* magazine. She is currently at work on a second racing-related Whitehorse Press project.

Laurel C. Allen

Mark Gardiner

Mark Gardiner was an ad agency creative director and amateur motorcycle racer for 15 years. In 2002, he quit his job, sold all his possessions, and moved to the Isle of Man to race in the TT. Since then, his motojournalist work has appeared in the magazines *Bike, Classic Bike, Performance Bikes, Cycle Canada, Road Racer X, Cycle World,* and a Swedish publication whose name simply cannot be pronounced at all in English. He is the author of the memoir *Riding Man.*

Mark Gardiner